What Country Is This?

What Country Is This?

John M. Weber

VANTAGE PRESS
New York

Cover design by Susan Thomas

FIRST EDITION

Published by Vantage Press, Inc.
419 Park Ave. South, New York, NY 10016

Manufactured in the United States of America
ISBN: 978-0-533-16141-6

Library of Congress Catalog Card No.: 2008908676

0 9 8 7 6 5 4 3 2 1

What Country Is This?

What country had over 2,200 infant deaths attributed to SIDS in 2002?

What country had 36% of its high school students saying that newspapers should get government approval prior to printing their stories?

What country issues $267,494 to the families of police officers killed in the line of duty?

What country had companies that paid $80,000 per second for their commercials to be aired during the 2005 Super Bowl?

What country had a company doing business in India that was responsible for its worst industrial disaster in history, who had to pay $470,000,000 to the families of the victims?

What country discovered that the largest segment of prisoners it imprisoned in Guantanamo, Cuba, after the Afghanistan war, were from the "friendly" nation of Saudi Arabia?

What country demanded from Saudi Arabia, and was paid, $50,000,000,000 for supplying armed forces to protect them from possible attack by Iraq during the Kuwait-Iraq-U.S. conflict?

What country was silent and remained friendly with Saudi Arabia, despite the fact that the Saudi government had beheaded over 60 rebels who had taken over a religious mosque?

What country threatened to invade Saudi Arabia in an effort to halt the oil embargo that King Faisal had imposed upon them in 1973?

What country has a state where more than 1,000 drivers were arrested for at least the sixth time, in the year 2000, for DUI?

What country, yearly, has hundreds of newborn infants who are abandoned and left to die by their young mothers, prompting some states to initiate programs whereby the infants can be dropped off at hospitals by their mothers, with no questions asked?

What country had a young man who hadn't even yet stepped onto an NBA basketball court when he was given a $90,000,000 contract by a sneaker company?

What country has the highest per capita imprisonment rate in the entire world?

What country had 70 major league baseball players fail their test for steroids in the year 2003 . . . even when they knew the tests were coming?

What country has about 1,250,000 of its citizens yearly, hear the dreaded notification that they have cancer.

What country has about 30,000 new products hitting the shelves every year, with a failure rate of about 90%?

What country had an average pay rate for a professional basketball player go from about $8,000 in 1954, to actually paying one player $28,000,000 for his 2005 season?

What country has over 150,000 students from China studying at their colleges and universities?

What country's federal agents received a tip that the Dillinger gang was hiding out in a restaurant building, and opened fire upon some diners who were leaving the restaurant, killing one and wounding another, while John Dillinger and his gang heard the shooting and escaped through a back door?

What country has a life expectancy of around 78 years while Zambia's life expectancy is 35 years?

What country experiences about an estimated 150,000 premature deaths yearly due to too much salt in its citizens' diets?

What country, in 1990, experienced 344 abortions for every 1000 live births?

What country had over 500,000 psychiatric casualties of service men during WWII?

What country butchers over 135,000 beeves for human consumption, yearly?

What country has suicides that exceed murders, yearly?

What country has a state that at one time sentenced 45 of 84 black men to death for rape convictions, but only 6 of 125 whites?

What country had 5 states, at one time, that banned the sale of contraceptives?

What country had 10,728 homicides due to handguns in 1981, versus Japan coming in a distant second with 48?

What country arrests over 640,000 people yearly for possession of marijuana?

What country's congress sent $117,000,000 to public schools that agreed to forego sex education, for teaching ''abstinence only'' in the year 2003?

What country had one city that put into effect a needle exchange program, and in one year had 250,000 needles exchanged?

What country has over 2,000,000 runaway kids, yearly?

What country has about 10,000,000 women on the pill and over another 11,000,000 who have been sterilized to prevent pregnancy?

What country has over 4,000,000 men who have chosen to have vasectomies?

What country had 1 in every 300 bankruptcies in the 70s and about 1 in every 70 in 2007?

What country has about 700,000 of its people having strokes, yearly?

What country refused to ratify the United Nations 1980 resolution outlawing the use of napalm and incendiary bombs against civilian populations?

What country has over 8,500,000 people getting some form of cosmetic surgery yearly?

What country had over 2,000,000 surveillance cameras in use in 2007?

What country has a win/loss soccer record with Mexico of wins–O, losses–22, ties –1?

What country has average salaries of white college-educated women at $37,761 and black college-educated women at over $41,000 in 2007?

What country paid the CEO of a company $51,600,000 for a year when the company actually lost $1,250,000,000?

What country has some 500,000 registered sex offenders walking the streets at any one time?

What country has a backlog of 500,000 DNA samples being tested involving over 52,000 murders, in 2007?

What country has 80,000,000 of its citizens suffering from the effects of hereditary hair loss?

What country allows the NFL to make only 1000 tickets to Super Bowls available to the public, and all of the rest go to "football insiders?"

What country has a prison population that is growing at a rate of 900 per day?

What country lost almost 25,000 soldiers in one Civil War battle called Shiloh in 1862?

What country has a former Secretary of Defense who visited Viet Nam many years after the war and asked a former Viet Cong general, "How could you sustain such large casualties, and continue on?" . . . to which the old Viet Cong general said simply, "It was our country."

What country had 120 SUV's in 2004 that backed over children, who were not seen by the drivers?

What country has about 1800 children dying in vehicle accidents yearly, of whom 900 of them were not using seat belts?

What country has around 500,000 people dying from cancer yearly?

What country has over 25,000 street gangs totaling about 750,000 members?

What country experiences almost 200,000,000 emergency calls to 911 yearly?

What country had over 5,000,000,000 credit card solicitations during 2004?

What country has over 400,000 knee operations being performed on overweight people, yearly?

What country has more than 75,000 kids ending up in emergency hospital wards due to trampoline injuries, yearly?

What country's government spent over $11,700,000 to drug test about 99,000 job applicants, only to find 153 who failed the test . . . costing the government about $77,000 each to determine who was using drugs?

What country lost about 6,000 ships in the Great Lakes, and 30,000 seamen during recorded history?

What country had 23,000,000 people in 2002 taking antidepressants?

What country has hospital-acquired infections affecting 2,000,000 people yearly?

What country and its allies had 45,000 airmen captured by the Germans during WWII?

What country has 65,000 illegal immigrants who graduate from its high schools yearly?

What country had students from an Arizona high school who entered an underwater robotics contest with many engineering universities, and won first prize, beating MIT . . . and all of those students were illegal immigrants?

What country had almost 8,000,000 of its citizens working two jobs to get by, in the year 1996?

What country has a large bank that processes about 40,000,000 checks per day?

What country has a government that disposed of about 10,000 computers every week?

What country has 53 million of its residents classified as "disabled"?

What country has 69,000 foreign born men and women on active duty in the armed services in 2007?

What country slaughtered an estimated 31,000,000 buffalo in the 19th century and had a pile of bones 12 ft. high that extended over 1½ miles?

What country imprisoned almost 18,000 California residents who were of Japanese ancestry, during the early days of WWII-... not to be released until the end of the war?

What country drafted boys of Japanese ancestry to fight in WWII at the same time as their mothers, fathers and families were in prison camps called "internment" camps in Arizona?

What country saw 24 boys of Japanese ancestry killed in action in the US armed services during WWII at the same time their families were situated in "internment" camps in Arizona?

What country experiences more than 1,000,000 vehicles stolen yearly, with an estimated 200,000 of them sent overseas?

What country has over 80,000,000 households making less than $25,000 per year in 2007?

What country purchased $185,000,000,000 worth of goods from China in 2004?

What country has 160,000 people visiting hospital emergency wards yearly for ladder-related injuries?

What country has about 400 marriages performed in prisons to inmates yearly . . . including some to serial murderers.

What country issues about 2,000,000 restraining orders to people yearly?

What country had a President (Lincoln) who put his 3 rivals for the Republican nomination for president into his cabinet?

What country had a president (Lincoln) who urged during his presidency that freed blacks should leave the U.S. for another continent?

What president (Lincoln) doubted the divinity of Jesus, and the infallibility of the Bible?

What country, in a medical study, denied nearly 400 black men in Alabama treatment for syphilis in order to determine the long term effects of the disease?

What country subjects about 100,000 psychiatry patients to electric shock therapy yearly?

What country has 3,000,000 kids being treated for ADHD in 2007?

What country experiences about 8000 venomous snake bites per year that result in an average of 12 deaths?

What country nabbed 45,000 recipients of federal SSI payments who were fugitives, in a program created in 1996?

What country kicked 3000 people out of their armed services in one year for getting too fat?

What country has an estimated 4.2% of its women suffering from bulimia?

What country has its citizens wagering around $760,000,000,000 yearly on gambling?

What country had 33 states in 2007 where at least some kind of gambling was legalized?

What country has estimated that 80% of the sun damage to skin occurs prior to the person's 18th birthday?

What country experiences at least 1,600,000 car accidents yearly involving trees, animals and vehicle debris . . . causing over 600 deaths?

What country has a deer population that has grown from about 500,000 to 30,000,000 over the past century?

What country's citizens lose an estimated 3,700,000,000 hours per year in traffic jams?

What country had 35 children die from being left in hot automobiles in 2004?

What country has lost an estimated 300,000 people due to asbestos?

What country has an estimated 97% of its population who do not follow the four rules of healthy living . . . eating right, keeping a healthy weight, exercising, not smoking?

What country has people spending over $48,000,000,000 on lottery tickets yearly, about $183 each for everyone in the nation?

What country has a large state that has among its residents, 102,000 registered sex offenders, about 18,000 residing in one county alone?

What country has an estimated 11,000,000 citizens with eating disorders such as bulimia and anorexia?

What country dismantled over 175 dams during the years 1999 through 2005?

What country has approximately 2,500,000 dams?

What country estimates that the cost of prosecuting a juvenile in criminal court ranges from $21,000 to $85,000?

What country went from 7,000 military pilots in 1940, to over 100,000 in 1942?

What country has more than 850,000 people having heart attacks, yearly?

What country has 48% of its adults in family households taking prescription drugs?

What country spends over $30,000,000,000 yearly on pet pampering . . . including such things as pedicures and massages?

What country had people buying 88,000 hybrid autos in 2004 . . . up ten times from the year 2000?

What country has 65% of its college graduates saying that they're headed back home to live with their parents?

What country's people have bought over 300,000,000 cell phones that can snap photos?

What country has 24,000 people learning the Chinese language of Mandarin, while China has 240,000,000 learning English?

What country has more Muslims living in it, than live in Afghanistan?

What country had over 10,000 Chinese immigrants working on the transcontinental railroad in the 1800s?

What country has an average consumption of sugared soda per person, at a level of 37 gallons (or 60,000 calories) per year?

What country refused to adopt the World Anti-Doping Agency's drug policy for its Major Leaguers and found its baseball team being dumped from the Olympics beginning in 2012?

What country has an estimated 67% of its dog and cat owners who regularly sleep with their pets?

What country has over 2400 hospital emergency rooms visits for oral injuries sustained during tooth brushing?

What country had the "take" from the gambling industry in 1996 at $47,000,000,000 increase to $73,000,000,000 in the year 2003?

What country had 38,000,000 hospitals visits during 2003, costing about $754,000,000,000?

What country has about 9,000,000 obese children in 2007?

What country lost over 50 journalists in the first two years of the Iraqi war?

What country loses roughly 500 people to carbon monoxide yearly?

What country experienced the rise in family healthcare premiums to be 6 times the rate of inflation between the years 2000 and 2004?

What country has 95,000,000 people turning to the internet for health information?

What country had one of the richest men in the world, J. Paul Getty, paying just $500 in income taxes in the early 60s?

What country had another of the world's richest men . . . H. L. Hunt, paying just $22,000 in income taxes in the early 60s?

What country has over 600,000 lightning strikes yearly, in one state alone?

What country has 47,000,000 medicare recipients in 2004, with another 10 million eligible, but not yet signed up?

What country has agreed to compensate Israel $150,000,000 for giving up their greenhouses in the Gaza strip when they turn the land back to the Palestinians?

What country has about one-third of all citizens covered by government health care . . . such as medicaid, medicare, federal employee, or military?

What country has 3.4% of its senior high school athletes who have admitted to using steroids?

What country has over 38,000 carjackings yearly?

What country lost over 1400 college students in the year 2004 due to alcohol-related incidents?

What country has one state where over 1300 public school teachers failed a state certification test 10 times or more?

What country has its children watching an average of 40,000 TV commercials per year?

What country uses an average of 6 times as much electricity per person as the average of the rest of the world per person?

What country has a large city that formed a ''cold case'' unit that was given 9000 unsolved murders dating back 4 decades?

What country had one city that had over 12,000 subway crimes reported in 10 months?

What country has about 125 people killed by avalanches yearly?

What country has over 50,000 shopping malls?

What country has the average net worth of black families at $6,000 and the average net worth of white families at $80,000?

What country exports about $60,000,000 worth of used clothes to Africa, yearly?

What country joined Britain and France in conducting atomic bomb detonations above and below some 250 islands in the Pacific since WWII . . . some where the residents were summarily removed?

What country has 16 countries ranked ahead of it when it comes to the international corruption perception index?

What country was fighting WWI in 1918 when the Spanish flu killed between 50,000,000 and 100,000,000 world-wide . . . more than three times those killed in the war?

What country has over 17,000 people waiting for liver transplants?

What country had 1 patient who had to pay $339,000 for a liver-transplant operation?

What country has about 28,000 people who go to work daily in the Pentagon?

What country has about 11,000 suicides on college campuses yearly?

What country had over 200 patients take advantage of the "Death with Dignity" Oregon law, up until the year 2005?

What country has over 12,000 miles of coastline?

What country's navy suffered hits on 300 ships from kamikaze aircraft during WWII?

What country lost every battleship it had in the Pacific ocean during the first 3 weeks of WWII?

What country discards over 2½ billion tons of clothing every year . . . about 5 to 1 women's clothes versus men's?

What country with an economy 5 times that of Germany discovered that Germany became the largest exporter of goods in the world?

What country went from under 300,000 consumer bankruptcies in 1980, to over 1,500,000 in the year 2004?

What country lost 670,000 people to the Spanish flu pandemic of 1918?

What country has more than 60,000 children removed from their own homes . . . for their own protection, yearly?

What country has over 1,100,000 lawyers?

What country in 2005 had over 1,500,000 adults taking medication to treat attention disorders . . . double that of the year 2000?

What country has over 34,000 registered lobbyists in Washington, D.C.?

What country has plastic surgery doctors working on the hands of some women, at a cost of over $4,000, to make them look younger?

What country had a woman who elected to have over 30 cosmetic procedures at a cost of over $80,000?

What country has provided a heart transplant for a convicted felon serving time for armed robbery, at an initial cost of $900,000?

What country provided dialysis treatments at a cost of $120,000 per year for a convicted murderer on death row?

What country consumes over $9,000,000,000 worth of bottled water yearly?

What country witnessed a 2,000% increase in heroin production from 2001 to 2005 while occupying Afghanistan, along with other UN countries?

What country releases about 800 people from one county jail every weekend day?

What country's taxpayers had to pick up the pension plan of a major airline after the airline declared bankruptcy?

What country elected one of the most popular presidents in history, who proceeded to oversee a 2 trillion dollar rise in the national debt, with tax cuts and spending on the military?

What country awarded a company (that its vice-president formerly ran) over $9,000,000,000 in contacts for the reconstruction work in Iraq?

What country purchased Alaska from Russia for the price of $7,000,000 in 1867?

What country tripled its border patrol in the 4 years after 9/11 to 2005?

What country allows 80% of the non-Mexicans caught crossing the border illegally to remain in its country while trials are scheduled . . . to which nearly no one ever appears.

What country fought the Japanese on the island of Iwo Jima during WWII, killing all but 200 of the 20,000 defending the island?

What country permitted Mexicans to enter it with just a payment of $8 during the early 1900s?

What country passed a law in 1882 excluding immigrants from China?

What country seized 300,000 pounds of cocaine coming into the country illegally, during one year?

What country passed a bill authorizing $5,000,000,000 for bicycle-friendly programs, in 2005?

What country has a major car-parts maker who has a $65 per hour average labor cost?

What country had over 94,000 reported rapes during 2004?

What country has a retired University professor who earns $272,000 in pension benefits per year?

What country had the number of company-sponsored pension plans drop from 112,000 in 1985 to just over 29,000 in the year 2005?

What country paid a CEO of a large company a lump sum pension of $33,200,000 after 25 years of service?

What country had a secretary and a policeman, living together in an apartment, who were going to spend the following on their wedding until the groom called it all off because the expense "got out of hand": $22,000 for renting the hall and the food, $14,000 for the ring, $5,000 for a video, $5,000 for photographs, $4,000 for the dress, and $2,000 for the disk jockey?

What country spends over $1,100,000,000 yearly for Halloween costumes?

What country has 16 states that do not allow Medicaid reimbursement for circumcisions?

What country in 1905 dispensed heroin and marijuana over the counter in local drug stores?

What country's citizens had a life expectancy of 47 years in 1905?

What country had only 8,000 cars in 1905?

What country's average wage was 22¢ per hour in 1905?

What country had 95% of its births taking place in the homes in 1905?

What country had only 14% of its homes with a bathtub in 1905?

What country has had its female prison population nearly doubled between 1995 and 2005?

What country has experienced one person who charged $241,000 to his American Express card during one night of excesses at a popular lap dancing site in a large city?

What country had over 478,000 liposuction procedures performed in 2004?

What country by 2005 had 230 cases of punishments meted out to U.S. service personnel related to the mistreatment of prisoners, including jail sentences, demotions, and other non-judicial punishments?

What country had over 500,000 premature births in the year 2005?

What country had an estimated 314,000 people who used heroin in 2005?

What country has 45 and older folks controlling two-thirds of all assets?

What country has 40,000 businesses that fail every month?

What country disposes of over 22,000,000,000 diapers yearly?

What country has an estimated 5,000,000 people with diabetes, who don't know it?

What country had candles that caused 18,000 fires and 130 deaths in 2002?

What country had a national conference in 1955 that concluded the number of illegal abortions being performed yearly was between 200,000 and 1,200,000?

What country has over 1,100,000 kids being home-schooled?

What country's National Weather Service regularly discouraged any tornado warnings reporting prior to 1950? (Their concern was to not encourage any panic.)

What country learned in 1994 that its citizens were spending as much on gambling as they were spending on groceries?

What country is it where women outlive men to the age of 95 by 4 to 1?

What country has a state where 840,000 out of 15,000,000 active licensed drivers have had a DUI conviction?

What country has in circulation over 1,600,000,000 credit cards?

What country has about 2,300 children who die from cancer yearly?

What country had over 12,000,000 of its citizens gambling illegally on the internet in 2006?

What country's citizens spent over $20,000,000,000 on anti-aging products in 2004?

What country's citizens purchase over 8,500,000 new vehicles yearly?

What country spends over $500,000,000 on Christmas trees every year?

What country will, in the next 10 years . . . release over 1,100,000 prison inmates into the population?

What country has an estimated 100,000 prison inmates who must spend 24 hours a day in their 8′ × 10 ′ cell, except for an hour or so three times a day to shower and exercise?

What country has over 11,000,000 citizens with food allergies?

What country has an estimated 7,300,000 couples who cannot have children?

What country has 16 states that require employers to have insurance that covers *in vitro* fertilization for infertile couples?

What country has about 2,500,000 people who are affected by anorexia?

What country had a church that was paid $30,000,000 for the "air rights" above its Manhattan church, which does not involve any construction in or above it?

What country's commercial fishermen toss 1,000,000 tons of fish overboard yearly, often because they are not the desired species?

What country has a Pentagon that spent $300,000,000 to plant rosy war stories in Iraqi newspapers?

What country has businesses and homes that dispose of 133,000 personal computers each day?

What country has aircraft that have to make forced landings, due to fumes or smoke in the cockpit, nearly once a day?

What country has 26 legal whorehouses in one state?

What country has over 20,000,000 people still wrestling with drug and alcohol addiction?

What country had 139,000 cases of heart attacks, strokes and other serious complications, linked to a medication before it was voluntarily withdrawn from the market?

What country had a reported 38,000 people put up $200,000 each in 2005 for a possible ride into space on a spacecraft that is being created?

What country spends about $44,000,000,000 yearly on its 15-agency intelligence community?

What country has a population of over 27,000,000 deer?

What country experiences about 1,500,000 collisions between deer and vehicles, resulting with approximately 200 people killed, yearly?

What country had 79,000,000 people who were eligible to vote . . . and didn't, in 2004?

What country has an estimated 12,000,000 people who contract a sexually transmitted disease, yearly?

What country has 60,000 people living in just one county, who have HIV?

What country has about 3,000,000 practicing Buddhists?

What country, on an average day, has 700,000 people who pass in and out of Grand Central Station?

What country saw a major league baseball pitcher with a losing record in 2005 . . . sign a five-year contract for $55,000,000?

What country has an estimated 4,200,000 people working exclusively from their home, and over 20,000,000 who work part time from home?

What country has 1 out of every 20 people who are illiterate?

What country had a law-enforcement group that spent $27,000 on a study to learn why inmates try to escape from prisons?

What country had a CEO of a large company who told a court that he "forgot" to declare a $25,000,000 bonus on his income tax form?

What country spends $102,000 to determine whether drunk fish are more aggressive than sober ones?

What country as of 2005 has had over 150 people convicted of serious crimes and then subsequently freed due to DNA test results?

What country has 4,600,000 unwed couples living together?

What country prevented Cuba's baseball team (a three-time Olympic champion) from entering the World Baseball Classic because of the embargo on the country?

What country has a magazine that is just intended for pro athletes that has in it for sale a $30,000 pair of sunglasses and a bed costing $64,000?

What country had a professional athlete who was caught at an airport checkpoint with a prosthetic penis designed to fool drug testing?

What country had a pro basketball player who said a $21,000,000 contract extension was not enough to feed his family?

What country has over 144,000,000 of its people with credit cards?

What country has over 20,000 people yearly who, during surgery, become aware while under anesthetic?

What country has about 13,000,000 smokers who try to quit yearly, with only about 3% succeeding?

What country has a hotel that offered a $3,000,000 New Year's Eve package that includes a car, expensive jewelry, a party, hotel rooms and much more for the celebration?

What country has over 2,500,000 infomercials shown on TV yearly?

What country has about 3,400,000 workers who spend a total of 3 hours or more per day commuting?

What country has one city that makes almost 4,000 prostitution-related arrests, every year?

What country had 216,000 veterans who received $4,300,000,000 in benefit payments for post-traumatic stress in 2004?

What country has more than 500,000 people with pacemakers?

What country has a huge company that has 6000 suppliers worldwide, and 80% of them are in China?

What country had an estimated 50,000 people who underwent lobotomies prior to 1967 when the practice was discontinued?

What country had almost 4,000 suicides among youngsters under 24 years old, in 2001?

What country had 50-yardline Super Bowl tickets in 1967 go for $12, and in 2006 go to $4,975?

What country spends about $33,000,000,000 yearly on diet books and diet-associated products?

What country's teens performed below the international average for 21 other countries, in general knowledge of math and science?

What country initially refused to allow a four-year-old boy on a commercial airline flight because his name matched one on the government terrorist list?

What country had a huge, successful multinational company freeze the employment retirement plans for 120,000 employees?

What country offers a hotel room outfitted especially for NBA players that costs $50,000 per night?

What country's president promised Joseph Stalin that his country would withdraw from Europe within two years after Hitler was defeated?

What country has an estimated 1,700,000 people over the age of 50 who are addicted to drugs . . . a number forecasted to triple by 2020?

What country had 2,233 indictments for public corruption between 2002 and 2006, making it the number one priority for the FBI's criminal division?

What country has about 700,000 people who suffer strokes yearly?

What country employs private contractors who pay their individual security specialists in Iraq up to $1000 per day for their services?

What country experienced online dating through internet personals grow from a $70,000,000 industry in 2000 to a $500,000,000 industry in 2005?

What country experiences over 250,000 truck accidents yearly?

What country experienced the deaths of 2,911 children and teen-agers by gunfire in 2001, and four times that many wounded?

What country has nearly 20,000 people who die yearly from radon-induced lung cancer?

What country has about 1/10th the population density of Japan?

What country is paying its auto workers about $65 per hour while the Chinese are paying theirs around $2 per hour?

What country has 13% of black males who marry outside of their race?

What country spends about $149,000,000 per year on home remodeling?

What country went from using about 4,000,000 barrels of oil per day in the late 70s to over 12,000,000 barrels daily in 2005?

What country, in addition to Libya, is the only country in the world to prohibit people with HIV from entering?

What country has over 1,500,000 vehicle accidents that are caused by distracted drivers . . . putting on makeup, eating, phone calls, putting in CDs, etc.?

What country spends over $10,000,000,000 on shaving and shaving supplies yearly?

What country decided not to help Egypt build its Aswan dam across the river Nile . . . leaving the door open for Russia to step in and help them bring electricity to hundreds of villages, and much-needed water for crops?

What country has an airline that decided to remove an olive from their salads served in first class, and thus saved $40,000 in one year?

What country has its elderly folks paying near $36,000 for assisted living facilities and an average of $74,000 per year for nursing home care?

What country had almost 8,000 people who turned 60 each day in 2006?

What country in the year 1900 had 1 woman in 20 in the workplace, and 1 in 4 in the year 1950?

What country ranks 25th in the world when it comes to 24-year-olds with science degrees?

What country imports some 70% of its cut flowers?

What country has over half of the people who are owed child support, not receive a single payment, in any specific year?

What country imports over 96% of its apparel?

What country has about 20,000 restaurants that go out of business yearly?

What country spent over $42,000,000,000 on women's shoes in 2005?

What country was responsible for "Operation Mongoose" that launched multiple covert CIA actions against Cuba?

What country has over 95% of its land . . . undeveloped?

What country has some men who earn up to $30,000 per year selling sperm to sperm banks?

What country had a president who vetoed a civil rights bill passed by his congress, shortly after the civil war? . . . only to have it overridden?

What country has an estimated 65,000,000 people with high blood pressure, and nearly one third are unaware of it?

What country has over 1000 "canned" hunting operations, in 26 states?

What country spent over $300,000,000 in 2005 trying to convince consumers that sleeping pills are safe and effective?

What country has a bill, sponsored by the NRA, that is before a state legislature that would make it a felony for an employer to forbid its employees . . . to take guns to the work site?

What country gives its Olympic gold medal winners $25,000?

What country gave out 75,000 emergency contraceptives (such as morning-after pills) in 1999, and 1,000,000 in 2004?

What country has women as the fastest-growing prison population in the year 2006?

What country has a large city that had 40,000,000 visitors to it in 2003?

What country had 21 military prisoners of the Korean war who refused to return to their homeland after the war was over?

What country had two so-called soldier "turncoats" who at the last minute changed their minds and decided to return to their homeland after the Korean war, only to be sentenced to prison terms of 10 and 20 years upon their return?

What country has a single county jail with a yearly budget of $400,000,000?

What country has an estimated 31,000,000 people who are hard of hearing?

What country has over 235,000 men diagnosed with prostate cancer, yearly?

What country found some 12,000 military aircraft stored underground in Japan at the end of WWII?

What country had a sitting vice president who once was quoted saying, that the vice presidency "wasn't worth a pitcher of warm piss?"

What country has a "working poor" population of nearly 45,000,000 people on medicaid, and more than 46,000,000 who have no health insurance?

What country seized over 135,000 marijuana plants being grown in one of their most northern states . . . on the West Coast?

What country had a bill before Congress in 2006 that would make it a Federal crime to "annoy" anyone on the internet?

What country had one large state that experienced 6,000 tornadoes over the past 50 years?

What country has discovered that alcohol-related car crashes cost about $45,000,000,000 per year?

What country's CIA covertly provided funds for Fidel Castro in 1952?

What country had over 400 church fires in the 90s that had to be investigated?

What country had a large city that planned to recycle cat and dog droppings by putting receptacles in parks, and then using the waste to process into methane gas?

What country had one military fighter squadron in Viet Nam that had 34 pilots out of 157 who were shot down?

What country had 73% of moms who were in the work force in 2000?

What country has more people killed in and by police vehicles, than by police guns?

What country has nearly 30,000,000 citizens who suffer from migraine headaches?

What country in the year 2006 announced that there was about $13,500,000,000 in matured government savings bonds, that went uncollected by their owners since 1941?

What country refused to renew a $48,000,000 grant to Brazil for AIDS prevention because Brazil would not formally state that prostitution is degrading?

What country passed a law in the early 1940s that allowed 5,000,000 Mexican workers into their country to replace farm workers who had been drafted into the armed services?

What country has handed out terms of up to 64 years in prison for individuals convicted of possession of cocaine with the intent to distribute?

What country has witnessed the production of 90% of the world's heroin still coming from Afghanistan four years after the Taliban was toppled?

What country sold 1,300,000 ''morning after'' pills in 2005?

What country had 2,500,000 people who applied for FEMA individual assistance after Hurricane Katrina struck Louisiana?

What country has one state with over 6,000 police car chases per year?

What country, in an out-of-court settlement, agreed to pay an Egyptian immigrant who was swept up after 9/11, $300,000, for detaining him for eleven months and denying him any legal representation?

What country has permitted over 600 members of congress to accept almost $20,000,000 for over 6000 privately-funded trips to travel, between 2000 and 2005?

What country has 581 prisoners on death in row in one state, waiting for their execution in 2006?

What country has about 3 times as many people carrying hepatitis C virus as are infected with HIV?

What country's government classified 15,600,000 "sensitive" documents in the year 2005?

What country initiated a program called "Safe Haven" that designated certain no-questions-asked drop-off spots for new mothers who don't want their babies . . . saving over 600 infants so far?

What country might have as many as 50,000 people involved in polygamous relationships, in one state?

What country found themselves fighting the French in Algiers during the Second World War, despite the fact that Germany had invaded France?

What country, overseeing the trial of Saddam Hussein in Iraq, has permitted a system to be installed and used, whereby the presiding judge can push a button that prevents the press and courtroom witnesses from hearing what the accused is saying?

What country has suffered over 38,000,000 young men wounded in wars, since the Revolutionary War?

What country has a huge retail company that paid their cashiers less than $12,000 per year on average, in 2005?

What country has the highest imprisonment rate in the world, while many other countries have just about one-fourth their rate?

What country has over 585,000 military veterans who have been convicted of a felony, and are therefore denied the right to vote?

What country increased its prison population by 1,600,000 between the years 1995 and 2005?

What country has their wealthiest 1% paying just 18% of their income in federal taxes, while the rest pay an average of 30%?

What country had corporations paying 30% of the total federal tax revenue in the 1950's, and in 2005 paying just 9%?

What country's federal budget contains about seven times as much of its military as for education?

What country owes $217,000,000,000 in interest to be paid in 2006 alone, its national debt of $8,200,000,000,000, with just about all of it accumulated since 1998?

What country's baseball team, entered in the World Baseball tournament, lost to South Korea, Canada, and finally Mexico, in 2006?

What country has over 30,000 babies born yearly who were conceived by artificial insemination?

What country's citizens pay almost $500,000,000 yearly for excess weight of their baggage, for commercial airline fights?

What country had a study done on lost airline luggage and estimated that 30,000,000 pieces of baggage are lost yearly?

What country's people spend over $2,500,000,000 yearly on the 3 most popular sleeping pills?

What country's citizens had over 108,000 facelifts performed in 2005 and 3,800,000 Botox treatments, along with over 1,000,000 chemical peels?

What country has a major automobile company that lost $10,600,000,000 in the year 2005?

What country lost over 2000 military aircraft during the Korean war?

What country experiences over 100,000 injuries on their golf courses, yearly?

What country had a CEO of a large aircraft manufacturing company who was ousted after serving just about 3 months for having an extramarital affair with an employee . . . earned over $11,000,000 during those 3 months, in salary and stock awards?

What country has a world-famous rifle manufacturer which had over 19,000 employees during WWII, down to 186 people in 2006, after being in business for over 150 years?

What country placed 19th out of 21 countries in student math proficiency?

What country has over 8,000 homeless people living in a 50-block area of one large city?

What country had a large auto manufacturer who has offered one type of buyout package to workers consisting of a $140,000 cash payment to those union employees who would give up their jobs and lifetime healthcare benefits?

What country's federal government refused to sign on to the 141-nation Kyoto agreement to reduce global warming, only to have mayors of 218 cities sign up for a commitment that meets or exceeds the Kyoto targets?

What country has a large retail company that saves an estimated $25,000,000 per year by having its truck drivers shut off their engines when stopped for a break?

What country performed Caesarean operations on over 29% of all births in 2006?

What country has almost 150,000 people treated yearly for head injuries suffered while riding bicycles?

What country has a state that sends undercover agents into taverns to arrest patrons for being drunk . . . resulting in over 2000 arrests in 2006?

What country budgeted $50,000,000 for making toy soldiers in an effort to stimulate and improve recruitment for the military services?

What country in the early 1800s built a prison that had central heating and flush toilets before they were even available in the White House?

What country passed a bill in Congress that provided $500,000 for a teapot museum?

What country's cigarette companies, due to a historic 1998 legal settlement, were going to pay about $5,300,000,000 to 46 states in 2006?

What country has over 90,000 people waiting for organs, not counting those needing corneas, heart valves, or tendons?

What country has 103 nuclear power reactors?

What country stood by in 1974 as India surreptitiously diverted plutonium from an intended peaceful-use nuclear test reactor that Canada was helping them to build, to set off an underground nuclear explosion?

What country suffered 23,000 killed and wounded in one day of fighting during its Civil War?

What country had about 100 kids in 2004 who contracted measles at the same time measles killed over 450,000 worldwide?

What country has over 12,000 nukes, and yet advises other countries that it's dangerous and immoral for them to attempt to acquire any?

What country had a budget of about $40,000,000,000 for its intelligence-gathering operations in 2005?

What country passed a law in 1986 that reduced the top tax rate for the wealthy from 50% to 28%?

What country has made some 15,000 changes to the tax laws since 1986?

What country has about 60% of all taxpayers who rely on professionals to do their income tax returns?

What country has about 30,000,000 people working full time, and still living in poverty, according to government standards?

What country's government learned that some Cubans were staying in a Sheraton Hotel in Mexico City and threatened the parent company of Sheraton with violating the U.S. sanctions against Cuba, because the parent company is an American entity?

What country's marriage rate dropped by about 50% from 1970 to 2005?

What country had a CEO of a company who exercised options for gains of nearly $250,000,000, which exceeded the annual profits of 550 of the Fortune 1000 companies?

What country has about 2,500 kids who drop out of high school daily?

What country has police arresting about 4,400 youths daily?

What country now has over 8,300,000 households with over one million dollars of yearly income?

What country had a large company that paid their stockholders $565,000,000 in a year when it was hemorrhaging cash and near bankruptcy?

What country locks up about 2,300,000 people every year?

What country has over 650,000 people released from its prisons and jails yearly?

What country has Britain voting most consistently with it on the UN security council, with China right behind?

What country has over 140,000 job applicants for its CIA yearly?

What country experienced a stock market day trader who went on a killing spree at his workplace that left nine dead and thirteen wounded?

What country experienced the slaughter of six and the wounding of nineteen in a commuter train when a gunman went berserk?

What country had a killer who fired upon 100 people who he didn't know, in a Luby's cafeteria, killing twenty-two before shooting himself?

What country experienced a shooting in a Mcdonalds where a man killed twenty-one people that he never knew, before a police sniper was able to shoot him?

What country has a population where only 6% normally use public transportation?

What country had its Internal Revenue Service (IRS) rules go from about 50,000 in 2000, to over 66,000 in 2005?

What country has a mall in one city that has 43,000,000 customers per year visiting it?

What country had a city whose archdiocese paid $150,000,000 during a three-year period in a legal settlement and other costs related to sex abuse by clergy members?

What country has estimated in 2006 that there may be as many as 500,000 sex offenders on the loose, and still wanted by law enforcement?

What country saw an oil company CEO retire in 2006 with a $400,000,000 pay and retirement package?

What country has 25,000,000 women 45 years and over, who are unmarried?

What country has almost 9,000,000 victims of identity theft yearly, allowing criminals to rip off some $56,000,000,000 in cash, goods, and services?

What country was involved in King Phillip's war of 1675 between the colonists and the native populations along the east coast, often described as one of the bloodiest wars the country ever had?

What country has 3,400,000 people who commute to work by driving 90 minutes or more, one way, in 2006 . . . double the rate of 1990?

What country had approximately 20,000 men who died in mining accidents in the 1920s?

What country loses about 800 children to swimming pool accidents yearly, and most are from drowning in back yard pools?

What country has at least three women who are murdered every day, by their husbands or boyfriends?

What country has from 200 to 300 children killing their parents, yearly?

What country has an estimated 75% of its taxpayers paying more into Social Security and Medicare taxes than they do in income taxes?

What country paid nearly $2,000,000 to a Mexican family because a Marine shot and killed a young boy near the Mexican border in a disputed incident?

What country loses $759,000,000,000 annually in productivity due to employees' personal internet usage while on the job?

What country had a western state unanimously pass a ''sedition law'' in the early 20th century that made it a crime to publish or say anything ''disloyal, profane, violent, scurrilous, contemptuous, or abusive'' about the government, soldiers, or the flag?

What country has a major city where 93% of those arrested never spend any prison time for their offenses?

What country has some 1100 college students who commit suicide each year?

What country has the second-highest infant mortality rate among industrialized countries, behind only Latvia, and loses about 10,000 infants within 30 days of their birth?

What country as 4,700,000 people, mostly children, who are bitten by dogs yearly?

What country, led by huge profits from stock trading and investment backing, provided $21,500,000,000 in record Wall Street bonuses in 2005?

What country had a high school that prohibited a twenty-one year-old Marine who had just returned from serving in Iraq, from taking his 18-year-old sweetheart to the senior prom? (The school bars prom guests older than 20, and refused to make any exception.)

What country has 25% of his physicians who get their M.D.s abroad?

What country charges about $50,000 for a heart by-pass operation, while in India, the cost would be about $8,000?

What country is seeing a stream of patients flying abroad to take advantage of surgeries such as for herniated disks that go for $90,000 at home, and can be accomplished abroad for around $9,400?

What country had a difficult time explaining democracy to the rest of the world after a presidential election that declared the winner was a man who received about 500,000 fewer votes than the loser?

What country pays its Presidents $400,000 per year and pays the commissioner of professional football about $10,000,000 per year?

What country has had studies where SIDS (Sudden Infant Death Syndrome) occurred some 50% of the time while parents were bed-sharing with infants?

What country, along with the rest of the international community, seems to have no plan to help the 850,000,000 people of the world who don't have enough to eat?

What country has up to 1,000,000 estimated cases of people living with autism?

What country has an estimated eight to twelve million people who are morbidly obese?

What country has about 45% of pregnancies unplanned?

What country spends something over $400,000,000,000 for their military, while a country like China spends about $35,000,000,000?

What country had a president who took a trip to East Africa and brought along 500 gallons of beer?

What country expended an estimated 75,000 to 100,000 rounds of M-16 ammunition for every enemy it killed in Viet Nam?

What country has an average of 10,000 complaints per day of mishandled luggage against their larger airlines?

What country has 456,000 youngsters ages 16 to 20 who were injured in vehicle crashes in 2004?

What country has about 90% of its people who do have HIV . . . don't know it?

What country had a shuttle accident during its 113th space flight where lives were lost and 84,000 pieces of debris crashed down, mostly over Texas?

What country took over the construction of the Panama canal after France lost 25,000 workers during their ten-year effort to build the canal?

What country has about 85% Christians, but only 28% who believe that the Bible is literally true?

What country has more gold deposited in the Federal Reserve Bank of New York than is in Ft. Knox, 78% of it owned by other countries?

What country arrested a man for pleasuring himself at a library while watching pornography on the internet, and was held on $500,000 bond?

What country prints 38,000,000 bank notes per day, of different denominations?

What country has a cost of 4¢ per bill, regardless of whether the denomination printed is of $1, $5, $10, $20, $50, or $100?

What country arrested almost 4,000 people in 1999 for counterfeiting?

What country has some $70,000,000,000 to $90,000,000,000 stored in a vault that covers 3 floors and is about the size of a football field?

What country has some $360,000,000,000 in currency stored in foreign countries?

What country decided in 1996 to redesign all bills except the $1 bill?

What country has some characters that measure just one one-hundredth of an inch on their bills?

What country can make 32,000,000 bank notes before wearing out the printing plates?

What country has just 13% of its nation's counties that have abortion clinics?

What country saw the average wedding dress size, double, in the 20 years leading up to 2006?

What country had an auto baron who attempted to build a rubber producing & processing plant in the Amazon and lost the equivalent of about $200,000,000 in the process?

What country sold the complete plans for the DC-3 aircraft to Japan, just a few years before the attack on Pearl Harbor?

What country still condoned slavery about 3 decades after it was forbidden throughout the British Empire?

What country had 2000 stabbings during one year in a large city jail?

What country turns away about 500,000 ambulances per year from hospital emergency rooms due to overcrowding?

What country had an estimated 1,000,000 "hobos" riding the rails during the height of the depression in the 1930s?

What country has an estimated $14,000,000,000 per year in auto insurance fraud?

What country has over 90,000 people waiting for lifesaving organ transplants?

What country had 9 of the signers of the Declaration of Independence belonging to the Freemasons, and there are nearly 2,000,000 of them in the country today?

What country has a major large city that has almost a 4 hour average wait for patients in its emergency ward?

What country, despite a ban on assault rifles, still had an estimated 4,000,000 in circulation in 2006?

What country had 217,000 hip replacement operations in 2003?

What country had 402,000 total knee replacements in 2003?

What country had a magazine that reportedly paid $3,500,000 for the first photos of a celebrity couple's newborn child?

What country arrested 2 women, ages 73 and 75, for perpetrating insurance fraud by allegedly taking out insurance on a homeless man and then arranging for his death?

What country has over 20,000 people afflicted with Lymes disease yearly?

What country's workers leave an estimated 574,000,000 days of vacation, untaken?

What country had 30% of all college students in the world in 1970, and just 14% in 2000?

What country has about 1,000,000 who die yearly in hospitals, of all causes?

What country had Indian gambling as a $20,000,000,000 enterprise about 3 times that of Las Vegas?

What country has the chance of being hit by lightning for one person, at 1 in 600,000?

What country joins China, Iran, and Saudi Arabia as the four countries that account for nearly all of the executions worldwide?

What country watched as the number of nations that abolished the death penalty over the past 30 years went from 16 to 86?

What country has put to death more than 1000 since 1976, and during that period 123 people on death row have been exonerated of their crimes?

What country between 2001 and 2006 has increased the number of Arabic speakers working for the State Department by just 33 people?

What country's post office delivers about 212,000,000,000 pieces of mail each year?

What country has about 94,000,000 people who plug into the internet each day?

What country has an average of 2,200 pieces of junk mail delivered to each person yearly?

What country gave some $10,000,000 to 1100 prison inmates who applied for disaster relief funds following hurricane Katrina?

What country has about 126,000,000 people who are exposed to second-hand smoke, leading to an estimated 50,000 deaths yearly?

What country contributes 45% of the world's carbon dioxide?

What country had over 26,000 cars and trucks abandoned in a city after hurricane Katrina, requiring them to be hauled away for salvage?

What country outnumbered the Spanish by over 10 to 1 in one of their most famous battles . . . the fight for San Juan Hill, in Cuba?

What country has over 880,000 physicians?

What country has a gay community that represents a $641,000,000,000 market?

What country has the average person moving about 11 times in a lifetime?

What country paid out $1,300,000,000 in subsidies to owners of farms, between 2000 and 2006 . . . for them agreeing to not grow crops?

What country had a hospital charge an uninsured patient $35,000 for an appendectomy, when the typical insured patient would have been charged about $7,000?

What country spent an estimated $4,200,000,000 on extended warranties for appliances and such, despite consumer reports that claim these are very poor investments?

What country paid out an estimated $4,200,000,000 in fees during 2005 for withdrawing cash from ATMs other than their own bank's ATMs?

What country discovered that 61% of its citizens did not know all of the words to their national anthem?

What country spent over $95,000,000,000 on their antiballistic missile system (''Star Wars'') between 1986 and 2006?

What country has about 76,000,000 ''baby boomers'' who retire in 2006?

What country had an average of 30,000 cigarette lighters confiscated every day from airline passengers at airport checkpoints?

What country has college students who borrow money to pay for college with an average debt of almost $20,000?

What country had a tsunami in 1964 that hit the West Coast and suffered 11 killed and millions of dollars in property damage?

What country has insurance fraud that costs the average family about $1000 per year?

What country has health insurance scams that amount to an estimated $50,000,000,000 in losses per year?

What country had a state police officer who arrested over 4,000 auto thieves during his 40-plus year career?

What country had 500 murders go unsolved in one city, during the period 1925 to 1932?

What country has NASCAR as its largest spectator sport?

What country had about 80% of its male population in the late 1800s smoking cigars?

What country has the odds of a child being afflicted with autism, of one in 166?

What country court-martialed over 600 service men and women on the battlefields of Afghanistan and Iraq between 2002 and 2006?

What country had just 1 in 16 people over the age of 65 in 1900, and almost 1 in 8 in the year 2000?

What country tried and convicted 122 of its own servicemen for killing civilians in Viet Nam during the war years?

What country has 9,000,000 adults who are at least 100 pounds overweight?

What country has an airport where over 2,000,000 hot dogs are sold yearly?

What country has an estimated 200,000 homeless veterans?

What country allows employers to fire their employees for any reason whatsoever, except in 5 states?

What country had a company who legally fired an employee for having a bumper sticker on her car for the ''wrong'' presidential candidate?

What country lost 241, mostly Marines, in a 1983 suicide attack on their barracks, in Lebanon?

What country in 2006 still had seven states where it was a criminal offense for a male and a female to live together without the benefit of marriage?

What country actually had 33 Republican congressmen who voted against renewing elements of the 1965 Voting Rights Act that was set to expire in 2006?

What country, in 1706, declared a woman a witch after she was cast in a river, and floated? Had she sunk and drowned, she would have been found innocent.

What country has about 1 in every 8 babies born prematurely?

What country has teen drivers crashing in their vehicles about ten times the rate of adults?

What country in 1944 had twenty-five German prisoners of war dig a 178' tunnel in the Arizona clay using spoons as shovels and escape with a prefabricated boat, only to reach the ''Salt River'' and find it completely dry?

What country has had studies that show France and three other European countries have more productivity per worker, per hour, than its own?

What country has a bridge that accounts for more suicides than any other place in the world?

What country passed a law whereby if a youngster is convicted of smoking a marijuana cigarette, he is prohibited from ever receiving any federal aid to his education?

What country will have an estimated 30,000 men's prostates removed by the use of robots in the year 2009?

What country's poor children, by the age of four, will have typically heard 32,000,000 fewer words than those whose parents are professionals?

What country has an estimated 100,000 convicted sex offenders who are supposed to be reporting where they live, but are unaccounted for?

What country has a list of about 200,000 suspected terrorists' names that is used to prevent their entering the country?

What country provided about $3,000,000,000 in gambling revenues to internet sources, until a 2006 law went into effect prohibiting it?

What country had a president shot in 1881, whose doctors treated the gunshot wound by inserting their fingers into it to determine the path of the bullet, and fed him rectally, leading to a loss of over 100 pounds until his death 80 days later?

What country had 3 of its top professional basketball players decline, in 2006, an invitation to play on its Olympic team?

What country experienced 141 deaths attributed to a heat wave, in just one state in 2006?

What country more than doubled the average size of a home, between 1950 and 2005?

What country spent over $4,200,000,000 on ATM charges in 2005?

What country launched a barrage of some 50 cruise missiles into a training camp in Afghanistan in an effort to kill Osama Bin Laden?

What country has about 1,000,000 students dropping out of school yearly?

What country has a city that is famous for gambling, that passed a law making it a crime punishable by six months in jail, if a person ''provides food or meals to the indigent for free,'' in its public parks?

What country has a prison population of which 75% are school dropouts?

What country has a golf club where the membership costs $600,000?

What country kills nearly 100,000 horses yearly for meat which it exports to Europe and Japan?

What country has over 1400 beer breweries?

What country, since 1978, has made it legal for people to brew beer in their homes?

What country routinely leaves estimated millions of citizens who have given up trying to get a job out of the unemployment percentage?

What country has 6,500,000 men and women receiving monthly disability checks of up to $1,000?

What country had a president in 2006 who signed over 100 bills that were passed by Congress, and added 807 so-called "signing statements" indicating what portions of the bills he interprets to be unconstitutional, and that he will not enforce?

What country had a judge in one state that denies asylum to about 96% of his cases, and a judge in another state who grants asylum to over 90%?

What country has a small charitable organization that developed a drug called paromomycin that might save up to 500,000 poor people per year; however, the large pharmaceutical companies decided not to pursue it, due to the limited profit potential?

What country has arrested 20,000,000 of its people for possessing or smoking marijuana, since it became illegal in 1937?

What country finds that 50% of all pregnancies are unintentional, and 60% of those occur when the woman is using birth control?

What country allows state governments to collect over $21,000,000,000 in cigarette taxes, yearly?

What country paid a CEO of a large drug company $148,000,000 in pay and pensions for five years of service, while shareholder assets plunged 43%?

What country has an estimated 40,000,000 people entering and leaving yearly?

What country's insurance companies get 2,000,000 claims yearly that involve minor neck injuries . . . mostly from rear-end vehicle accidents?

What country, in July of 2006, had 570,000 houses in stages of foreclosure?

What country's top 10 serial killers have killed 260 people?

What country fined a large pharmaceutical company $70,000,000 for overcharging for drugs, only to have a company spokesman say the payment was "non-material" to the company?

What country has about 50% of the children who are in foster homes in one state, there due to methamphetamine use by their parents?

What country has vetoed resolutions in the United Nations over 70 times where the countries voting for the resolution numbered over 100, and the countries agreeing with their veto was one or two?

What country passed a law in 1906 making it illegal for the manufacturers of Coca-Cola to use cocaine as an ingredient in their soft drink?

What country consumed 5 times as much alcohol per person in the 1850s as in the year 2005?

What country had the signers of the Declaration of Independence who did not reveal their names until the following year . . . in fear of the British punishing them as traitors?

What country has 14,000,000 people daily riding subways, busses, and commuter trains?

What country's commercial airline industry lost $40,000,000,000 in the five years following the 9/11 tragedy?

What country has 80% of all of its refrigerators with baking soda inside?

What country has experienced over 75 votes in the entire United Nations assembly where all of the other countries voted for a matter before it, and it was the lone country voting against the matter?

What country, after an impressive TV advertisement campaign, has sold over 10,000,000 packages of a compound for "male enhancement?"

What country discharged over 11,000 gays from the military from 1994 to 2005?

What country won all of its Olympic basketball games in 1992 by an average of 44 points, only to experience losses to Puerto Rico and Argentina in the 2004 Olympics?

What country lost 40,000 people due to car crashes in 2005, and zero due to terrorists?

What country had 768 children under the age of 13 murdered in 2004?

What country made more light machine guns in one month during WWII, than Japan did during the entire war?

What country has one community of 39,000 where half of all black men are either in prison, on parole, or on probation?

What country spends about $4,000,000,000 per year gassing up its warplanes?

What country, during a great river flood in 1927, rounded up black people at gunpoint who were needed to shore up the levees?

What country spends as much on pornography as it does going out to the movies?

What country had about nine times the number of women in prisons in 2004 than there were in 1977?

What country approved about half of the soldier applications for conscientious objector status, between 2003 and 2005?

What country had to discipline 80 military recruiters in 2005 for sexual misconduct?

What country is home to some 10,000 tigers . . . owned by individuals and zoos?

What country had Alien Land Laws in the early 1900s that prevented foreign born ''orientals'' from owning land?

What country lags far behind China as the world's largest steel producer?

What country had a person rise to be attorney general of a state, with a past record of 12 speeding tickets, 4 bench warrants, and 3 drivers license suspensions?

What country had 432,000 people who finished a marathon in 2005, up from 25,000 in the year 1976?

What country had a state that passed a law outlawing french fries, whole milk, candy bars and soda pop, in their elementary and middle schools?

What country had more than 200 people who ''confessed'' to the Baby Lindbergh kidnapping?

What country had an executive from a company that makes bulletproof vests for the military, who paid a reported $10,000,000 for a bat mitzvah celebration for his daughter?

What country has more black men in prison than in college?

What country pays its professional golf caddies up to $750,000 for a thirty-two-week year?

What country continued to ignore payment of its United Nations dues until it was $1,800,000,000 in arrears and was threatened with losing its vote on the Security Council?

What country objected to Israel's use of American-made cluster bombs against Lebanon in 1978 and 1982, and restricted their use to ''hard'' targets as opposed to areas inhabited by civilians?

What country objected to Israel's massive air strike against Iraq's nuclear research installation?

What country has butterfly farms that ship about 11,000,000 butterflies for classrooms and weddings and such, yearly?

What country had 55,000 people over the age of 100, in the year 2005?

What country has one state that is comprised of 43% Hispanics?

What country had 79,000,000 people who didn't vote in the 2004 election?

What country's military told the families of two National Guardsmen who were killed in June 2004, by the Iraqi civil-defense soldiers they were training, that they were killed in an enemy ambush . . . and it was two years before the families were told the truth?

What country laid off nearly one-half of the IRS auditors who examine the estate tax returns for the wealthiest taxpayers, in 2006?

What country had 250 unsolved murders in one city in 2005?

What country has an estimated 18,000 people who die yearly due to not having any health insurance?

What country's military mistakenly paid about $900,000 to 75 army reservists who were designated deserters for failing to report for duty after 9/11?

What country had a large city that outlawed the sale of foie gras (fattened livers of ducks and geese) from restaurants?

What country federally outlawed the growing of hemp because of its genetic similarity to marijuana, but continued to allow its importation from Canada?

What country has some 85% of all cigarette smokers smoking supposedly "safer" cigarettes, and 95% of them compensating by inhaling more deeply, taking more puffs, or smoking more cigarettes?

What country had 4553 highway deaths due to motorcycles in 2005?

What country has about 1,500,000 people who suffer from Parkinson's disease?

What country has about 60,000,000 people who legally cross back and forth its border at just one city, per year?

What country has roughly half of all of all TVs sold, assembled in one city south of the border?

What country began vaccinating youngsters in the 1960s when the rate of German measles was about 33,000 per 1 million people, and reduced it to 2 people per million?

What country had one city where 122,000 marriages took place in the year 2005?

What country has volunteers who contribute an estimated $150,000,000,000 in economic manpower value yearly, to worthy causes?

What country imports many goods from China where the average wages average only about 2% of those in its country?

What country spent just $8,000,000,000 for economic reconstruction and infrastructure in Iraq, of the total of $300,000,000,000 spent during the first three years of the war?

What country has legalized prostitution in some areas of one state?

What country has some 96% of prison convicts who will be back out on the street someday?

What country seized and took over a brothel for unpaid federal taxes, and put it up for auction?

What country has a population of some 200,000 black bears?

What country created a $200,000,000 so-called "Coalition Solidarity Fund" that paid countries like Albania $6,000,000 for its contribution of 155 soldiers to the Afghanistan and Iraq wars?

What country pulled itself out of the ABM treaty and is spending $9,000,000,000 on its missile defense system in 2006 and the same in 2007?

What country's research has determined that how tall your parents were explains some 90% of how tall you are, but how long your parents lived explains only about 3% of how long you will live?

What country gives away about $10,000,000,000 in foreign aid yearly, plus what is given to Israel and Egypt agreed to in the Camp David accords?

What country has over 6,000,000 children who suffer from asthma?

What country, had the city fathers of a large coastal city use the 1906 earthquake as an excuse to drive out all Chinese immigrants . . . and would have been successful had not the state governor intervened?

What country comes in second to Turkey out of thirty countries surveyed to see how many people do not believe in evolution?

What country regularly distributes 300,000,000,000 coupons annually, with about 99% ending up in the trash?

What country has 23,000,000 households headed by someone over 65?

What country had a small agency in the Treasury Department track down a woman who had gone to Cuba to pass out free Bibles, and when she returned, advised her they intended to fine her $10,000 for unauthorized travel to Cuba?

What country pays a golfer an estimated $85,000,000 yearly for endorsements, in addition to the $70,000,000 he has earned over the years playing golf?

What country has women consuming about two-thirds of all chocolate sold?

What country tried to kick John Lennon out of the country for speaking out against the Viet Nam war, only to have the courts allow him to stay?

What country paid families of victims of the 9/11 attack, up to $4,100,000?

What country has nearly half of all prison inmates who are released on parole, ending up back in prison within the first year?

What country experiences some 90% of the deaths from hurricanes, from drownings?

What country, during the great flood of 1927, saw some levees in New Orleans intentionally dynamited to flood some areas of the city, and to save other areas.

What country found that overall compensation costs were 46% higher for state and local governments than for the private sector employers, in a 2005 survey?

What country has experienced 30,000,000 people being laid off from their jobs in the two decades prior to 2006?

What country's Olympic basketball team, comprised of many of the best professional athletes, finished 6th in 2002 and was beaten by Greece in 2006?

What country had a base minimum starting salary for major league baseball players, of $327,000 in 2006?

What country's government accounted for 67% of total research and development spending in 1967, which has fallen to about 30% in 2006?

What country had an average time per household of watching TV of 8.2 hours in 2005?

What country's average waistline grew 1½ inches between 1988 and 2002?

What country has about 90% of men in their 70s and 80s with symptoms of an enlarged prostate?

What country's army in 1938 was smaller than that of Finland?

What country imposed upon Japan in 1947, Article 9 to their constitution which states, ''The Japanese people forever renounce threat or the use of force as a means of settling international disputes''?

What country leads all others by a wide margin in the sale and export of small arms, with around $533,000,000 yearly?

What country has lobbyists who spent $2,400,000,000 in their nation's capital in 2005?

What country has 61 registered lobbyists for every single member of Congress?

What country has an estimated $1,000,000,000 worth of prescription drugs being flushed down the toilet yearly, or otherwise unused and discarded?

What country's women over 50 will experience a broken bone due to osteoporosis in their lifetime?

What country loses around forty lives annually to white-water rafting accidents?

What country had 10,000 people who filed workman's compensation claims resulting from respiratory problems resulting from their work on ''Ground Zero'' reclamation?

What country has set aside 106,000,000 acres as permanent wilderness, where all commercial activity is prohibited?

What country has an AIDS infection rate in prisons that is nearly five times that of the general population?

What country's Social Security Administration receives over 8,000,000 earnings reports from the IRS that are filed under names that do not match the Social Security numbers, annually?

What country had over 95% of all births taking place in the home in 1906?

What country had only 6% of all its citizens, high school graduates in 1906?

What country had only 230 reported murders in its entire country in 1906?

What country has some 21,000,000 people who suffer from depression?

What country did not allow any blacks to play major league baseball until 1947?

What country has one company with over 3,000 stores, that are visited weekly by roughly the equivalent of one-third of the population of the country?

What country estimates that it had $345,000,000,000 of unpaid federal income taxes in 2001?

What country permits each of its 50 states to have just 2 statues in their state capitals?

What country has a national park that experiences about 1000 cars broken into by bears, every year, looking for food?

What country has mined only about 10% of its known copper deposits?

What country gets a yield of 6 pounds of copper for every 2000 pounds of copper ore?

What country uses about 200,000 pounds of copper in each of its nuclear submarines?

What country's FDA has fined the Red Cross $9,700,000 between 2003 and 2006 for various violations related to their handling of donated blood?

What country is prosecuting a man who may have evaded some $200,000,000 in federal and other taxes?

What country has a state that has prohibited anyone convicted of a crime ''or moral turpitude'' from voting, and has interpreted this to include a DUI conviction, among others?

What country had a naval fighter pilot during the Viet Nam war who was shot down and taken prisoner, and was later offered to be freed because his father was an admiral . . . but astonishingly, he refused?

What country lost 2,500 service personnel during the attack on Pearl Harbor on December 7th, 1941?

What country showed newsreel footage of their planes strafing the enemy survivors of ships sunk in the Pacific?

What country had 750,000 people who purchased highway motorcycles in 2004 for a total of $7,600,000,000?

What country in 2006 reportedly is holding some 13,000 men in prisons around the world, but mostly in Iraq, and has released around 18,000 over the past few years?

What country had a public health survey that determined that 150,000 lives could be saved annually if salt levels in packaged and restaurant foods were cut in half?

What country has some 90,000,000 people members of Costco and Sam's Club?

What country has banned the importation of oil from Iran since 1979?

What country has a cheerleader mom who tried to hire a hit man to murder the mother of her thirteen-year-old daughter's cheerleader rival?

What country had a second string kicker on a college football team who stabbed the starting kicker in the leg, ostensibly so he could take his place?

What country had a survey in 2006 where over 40% believed that they were in the last days of the world?

What country has an estimated 120,000 Muslims in its prisons?

What country has about 20% of its corporations that allow dogs in the office?

What country had a run on Wheaties when it was rumored that Frank Sinatra ate them to increase his sexual prowess?

What country had a study that found the average salary of working men who drank alcohol is 10% higher than those who did not drink . . . and with women, the figure is 14% higher?

What country had a record set in 2005 when 1355 CEOs departed from their companies?

What country had over 8,000,000 acres burnt by fire in 2006?

What country has purchased over 250,000,000 Monopoly games over the years?

What country passed a law in one state that allowed 150 new mothers to abandon their infants at certain designated places without any penalty during the first 5 years after enactment?

What country's pharmaceutical companies gave away over $5,000,000,000 worth of medicines, in 2006?

What country arrested 25 illegal workers at their work place in 2002 and over 600 in 2006?

What country had 90,000 people who entered the lottery for 50,000 spots in a large city's marathon race?

What country witnessed a forty-second standing ovation at the United Nations for a speech delivered by a Venezuelan president where he called its president "the Devil"?

What country has an estimated 100,000 patients who undergo shock therapy (ECT) yearly?

What country has a $1,600,000,000 "business" of mandatory hotel and motel extras such as charges of $1 per night for one night's telephone service?

What country has discovered that 1100 laptop computers are missing and presumably stolen, since 2001, from the Commerce Department?

What country has more TVs in homes than people?

What country is having a $200,000,000,000 class lawsuit filed against two huge tobacco companies for marketing so-called "light" cigarettes as safe?

What country has an estimated 2,000,000 people who self-mutilate?

What country has a so-called ''No Child Left Behind'' law that requires that military recruiters be allowed on high school campuses?

What country dumped 2,000,000 old vehicle tires into the Atlantic Ocean in an effort to seed an artificial reef, only to have to spend an estimated $5,000,000 to remove them some 35 years later?

What country has 50,000,000 people suffering from insomnia and other sleep disorders?

What country had the CEO's board of directors of a huge communication company cut the annual pay from $56,000,000 in 2004, to $21,000,000 in 2005, and recommended $10,000,000 in 2006?

What country has found that allergies cost the economy about $18,000,000,000 in lost productivity, yearly?

What country has had over 700,000 people who have had gastric by-pass surgery costing each of them around $80,000?

What country had a prison where an outbreak of violent fighting took place between Hispanics, whites, and blacks, in the prison yard, and after it was all over, officials found a total of 87 knives and sharp objects that had been used?

What country lost 65 women in the military who died in conflicts in Iraq and Afghanistan during the first 3½ years?

What country, after learning that some 600 marriages take place in a popular national park yearly, instituted a $50 charge for anyone who wants to say ''I do'' under the stars?

What country has found that head lice accounts for up to 24,000,000 missed school days annually?

What country had the average woman giving birth to 7 children in the early 1800s?

What country had a population of just 100,000,000 in 1915?

What country has a white population that's a minority in 4 states?

What country lost 763 servicemen in the torpedo sinking of the SS Leopoldville just five miles off of the coast of France, on Christmas Eve, 1944?

What country provided Iran with a $200,000,000 grant in the mid-1950s for the purchase of military weapons?

What country supported Iraq in its war against Iran in the 1980s, even after it was known that Iraq was using chemical weapons leading to the death of an estimated 50,000 Iranian soldiers?

What country has its Society of Civil Engineers who say there is a need for $1,600,000,000,000 above what is currently budgeted, for the maintenance and repair of dams, bridges, roads, power grids, and sewers?

What country has had nearly 400 school kids killed in school by stabbings and shootings, between 1990 and 2006?

What country has a large state that has 500,000 real estate agents?

What country has had a study that determined the average woman speaks about 20,000 words per day and the average man, just 7,000?

What country will be paying about $350,000,000 per plane for the new F-22 fighter jet, including development costs?

What country is paying $11,500 for the average cost of family health insurance in 2006, up from about $100 per person in 1950?

What country lost 22 of 28 gold matches in Ryder Cup play in 2006, allowing Europeans to win 5 of the last 6?

What country has a radio broadcast with a budget of $38,000,000 that beams an anti-Castro propaganda message from an aircraft flying at 20,000 feet, in an attempt to avoid Cuba's efforts to jam it?

What country has 13,900,000 people employed in private health services, and just 14,200,000 in manufacturing?

What country had two players vying for baseball's major league MVP, with one of them earning $20,600,000 per year and the other just $355,000?

What country has one large state with 2,300 justices presiding in local courts, but only 400 of them are certified lawyers?

What country has about 20,000 people being treated with a cancer drug that costs $4,200 per dose, and has not been proven to prolong survival?

What country has a medicare population of 42,500,000?

What country has nuclear power that supplies one-fifth of the nation's energy?

What country has a child's odds of becoming a professional athlete set at about 16,000 to one?

What country has one in every 20 child being cared for by a nanny?

What country has 44% of their colleges that accept every single applicant?

What country had a woman confidentially confess to her minister that she had an affair, only to have him tell his entire congregation about it, and ordered her shunned?

What country has over 8,000,000 RVing households?

What country has almost 66% of high school graduates who go on to college, but has over 40% dropouts there?

What country has over 2500 four-year colleges and universities?

What country's FDA allows any person or company to file a petition challenging generic drug approval, thereby delaying approval of the low-cost generic version until after a lengthy investigation is completed?

What country went from a maternal death rate in the early 1900s of 1 in 100, to 1 in 100,000 in 2006?

What country has 80% of the women in some prisons, there for drug-related crimes?

What country has over 31,000,000 who suffer form hearing loss?

What country has about 2,000,000 kids who run away yearly?

What country has just barely 1% of women in prisons who have visitors on any given day?

What country has women in one medium-sized prison who give birth to about 175 babies per year?

What country has 70% of all black children being born to unwed mothers?

What country has more than nine out of every ten schools where junk food is for sale?

What country had over 12,000 cases of sexual harassment in the workplace in 2005?

What country has an average child who witnesses about 200,000 acts of TV violence prior to age sixteen?

What country, according to a Pentagon study, has 1800 Wiccans in the armed forces?

What country has the largest seller of aspirin, Bayer, a German company?

What country has 28 states that have banned corporal punishment, but had over 300,000 school kids who were disciplined with it, in the school year 2002–2003?

What country has eight wounded for every soldier killed in Iraq . . . twice what it was in Viet Nam?

What country had a recently published book that made the dire forecast that 4% of teenagers will be ''Bible-believing Christians'' as adults, if current trends prevail?

What country arrested a man for being ''verbally abusive'' to the administration's vice president . . . only to drop the charges later?

What country in 1935 lost a huge dirigible in the ocean off its west coast that was 3 times the length of a 747, and the most expensive aircraft ever built at the time?

What country during WWII "interned" about 2,500 Japanese-Americans into one of 10 such camps, and required them to work 7 days a week, 12 hours a day, at a vegetable processing plant, for 55¢ an hour?

What country set aside $20,000,000 in a military spending bill in 2006, to pay for a celebration in the nation's capitol, for victory in Iraq and Afghanistan?

What country is it more likely to have a murder in Orlando, than in New York City?

What country presided over Iraq as Iraq passed a law that punished anyone who "publicly insults" the government or public officials, with seven years in prison?

What country has about 44,000 people on its "no-fly" list as of 2006?

What country has 21% of its home buyers represented by single women?

What country has $1,800,000,000,000 in credit card debt.

What country has an estimated 50,000,000 people suffering from chronic pain?

What country has at least 18,000 people who die annually of heart attacks because they didn't receive preventive drugs?

What country has 1,500,000 people who are harmed annually due to medicative errors, costing about $3,500,000,000 to treat the injuries created by those errors?

What country put the President of Bolivia on its secret "no fly" list?

What country has General Electric with 10,400,000,000 shares, while General Motors has only 566,000,000?

What country has an average citizen consumer who burns 26 barrels of oil per year, versus the average European 12?

What country has about 220,000 private aircraft?

What country has paid about $77,000,000,000 in interest to foreign creditors in China, Japan, and elsewhere?

What country had a president's wife who saw her son decapitated in a train accident?

What country has a President's ''cabinet'' that is not mentioned in its constitution?

What country had a president whose wife held 392 news conferences during his presidency?

What country had an incapacitated president, whose wife effectively took over in the early 1900's?

What country received just one-seventh of the Negro slaves from Africa that Brazil received?

What country's people can save about 80% of many medical expenses by traveling to India for comparable surgeries?

What country has the top 1% of wealth holders having about one-third of all wealth?

What country had the average income of the highest-paid officers at major corporations rise from $850,000 in 1970, to $4,600,000 in 2005?

What country had less than 50% of 111,000,000 households made up of married couples in 2005?

What country considered Sweden, Canada, and France as the top nuclear proliferation threats in the 1950s?

What country's Yankees baseball team did not win a World Series between 1978 and 1996?

What country has Wyoming as the leading state in average annual giving to charities?

What country has two states that have no voting restrictions for past criminal records, and even allows prison inmates to vote?

What country has 5,300,000 people who are denied voting rights because of criminal records?

What country has 16 states that have recently loosened voting restrictions on felons, restoring voting rights to about 600,000?

What country has a large city with 8,000,000 people, and 1,500,000 are poor?

What country has just 7% of all child molesters, strangers . . . the vast majority are family members?

What country has a major commercial airline that has slashed its fleet from 626 in 2000 to just over 400 in 2006?

What country has over 67,000 people on a waiting list for a new kidney in 2006?

What country accounted for 70% of the global airline market in the 1970s, down to just over 40% in 2006?

What country taxes gasoline at about 40¢ a gallon while Britain and France tax around $4.00 per gallon?

What country has about one-third of its population on 5 or more medications?

What country has a new baby born every 7 seconds?

What country had over 185,000 people bumped from airline flights in the spring of 2006?

What country has just 33 FBI agents with a limited proficiency in Arabic, and none that are equal to those of a native Arabic speaker . . . out of about 12,000 agents?

What country has had thirty consecutive years of trade deficits?

What country has sold over 60,000,000 books on the fictionalized accounts on the coming end of the earth?

What country's number one killer of teenagers is car crashes?

What country's average new home in 1950 had about 950 square feet, and in 2006, over 2,400 square feet?

What country will have some 270,000 diagnosed with breast cancer a year, with about 41,000 dying of advanced disease?

What country makes over 500,000 arrests of illegal immigrants yearly?

What country experienced 370 deaths due to defibrillators that didn't work?

What country went from 1,700,000 juvenile arrests in one year, to 2,700,000 three years later?

What country's Coast Guard now has boat-mounted machine guns on its ships in the Great Lakes, for the first time since an 1817 treaty was signed?

What country has one state that released some 127,000 prison inmates in 2006, and about 83,000 returned within the next three years?

What country had about 25,000 prison inmates taking part in prison college programs in 1994, only to have Congress remove them from Pell Grant eligibility, abruptly ending their education?

What country had 152,000 people prior to 2002, who tried to evade paying millions of dollars in federal income taxes, claiming that most citizens are not required to pay them . . . and by 2006 just eight have been convicted?

What country has a major commercial airline that receives about 230,000 phone calls per day?

What country has a major airline that changes its fares tens of thousands of times per day?

What country has a major airline that charges up to 66 different fares on a typical commercial airline flight?

What country, in 2006, had the only major airline that has never filed for bankruptcy, and yet has lost over $8,000,000,000 over its lifetime?

What country has a large city that has a policy of thoroughly investigating all complaints of police misconduct, and has experienced thousands of complaints from gang members who are taking advantage of this policy?

What country has 60% of unplanned pregnancies occurring in women who are using contraception?

What country has 66 registered lobbyists for every member of Congress in 2006?

What country signed a bill into law in 2006 that had 6,000 so-called ''pork barrel'' ear-markers in it?

What country spent about $2,600,000,000 on the 2006 elections?

What country had 2% of interest-only loans for homes in 2000, and 33% in 2006?

What country had stock in a textile company in 1962 that was selling for $7 per share, and in 2006 is selling for over $100,000 each?

What country has 75% of their female inmates . . . mothers?

What country has over 300,000 children who have mothers in prison?

What country consumes just half as much beer per person as the Czech Republic?

What country has immigrants from Latin countries sending an estimated $45,000,000,000 back to their countries annually?

What country has a men's wear designer who sells his basic men's suits for an average of $3,500 each?

What country has a former CEO who was paid $85,000,000 after less than a year on the job, and was removed for failing to improve the company's stock price?

What country passed a law intended to impede online gambling that was responsible for an estimated $23,000,000,000?

What country allows first cousins to marry in about half of its states?

What country has annual sales of $12,200,000,000 for a drug that is used to reduce cholesterol?

What country is spending $380,000 for every minute it stays in a war in Iraq?

What country is offering reenlistment bonuses that in some exceptional circumstances reach $150,000?

What country had a judge rule that a top executive must return $100,000,000 of his compensation, as being too excessive?

What country has over 2,600 service men and women who have had their security clearance revoked for being too much in debt . . . thus preventing them from being deployed overseas?

What country experienced autism at a rate of 1 in every 2,500 in 1970, and a rate of about 1 in 170 in 2006?

What country has new uniforms for military service personnel that includes a patch the size of a postage stamp with a unique infrared signature that helps to determine friend from foe?

What country experienced deaths due to friendly fire at a rate of 10% in Viet Nam, and 17% in Operation Desert Storm, as compared to deaths inflicted by the enemy?

What country has had the average woman weighing 20 pounds more in 2006 than she did in 1976?

What country has nearly 12,000,000 people with at least one tattoo?

What country hired its first black NBA basketball player in 1950?

What country's Supreme Court issues just about 40% of its decisions as unanimous?

What country installed more than 1,500,000 stents in the year 2006 alone?

What country has one city that issues over 9,000,000 parking tickets per year?

What country has scofflaws who receive parking tickets in one city, and fail to pay for them in the amount of $245,000,000 per year?

What country has twice as many suicides as homicides?

What country's people donated over $62,000,000,000 to the 400 largest charities in 2005?

What country has over 162,000 people dying from lung cancer, annually?

What country had over 47,000 people over 65 enrolled in college in 2004?

What country has over 236,000 farms being owned and run by women?

What country has less than 1% of its farms and ranches owned by non-families?

What country has average daily purchases of Budweiser Light beer of over 35,000,000?

What country has average daily purchases of Trojan Ultra thin condoms of over 123,000?

What country has over 97,000,000 of its people over 12 who have used marijuana at least once?

What country would a married couple with one high lifetime earner and a stay-at-home spouse have to shell out over $700,000 to buy a benefit to match what Social Security pays?

What country has nearly 20% of its Christians who speak in tongues more than several times a year?

What country has a famous NFL football coach who has fourteen assistants, and another eighteen trainers and support staff under him?

What country has a National Football League that received $3,700,000,000 from TV networks in 2006?

What country has about 1 in every 100 affected with schizophrenia?

What country has 17,000 children hurt in school bus accidents annually?

What country has its typical Harley-Davidson motorcycle buyer at age 47?

What country has one large company that spends an estimated $570,000,000 on advertising?

What country had a president who weighed 320 pounds?

What country has a program that distributes surplus "as-is" military hardware such as M-16, F-16s, body armor, helicopters, and armored personnel carriers at no cost to friendly governments, and in 2006 the giveaways and, sometimes, sales of 5¢ on the dollar, amounted to $1,560,000,000?

What country had a major league baseball team that had to pay a fine of over $35,000,000 for going over their league-imposed salary cap?

What country had 185 prison inmates serving time for rape that were cleared due to results of DNA testing?

What country's gas prices waver between $2 and $3 per gallon at the same time Venezuela's price is 12¢ per gallon?

What country has a large company that regularly sends its employees out to competitors' stores, to insure that their own prices remain the lowest?

What country had the religion of the Mormons start a city in the desert with 148 people in the 1800's, and see it grow to over 700,000 in the late 20th century?

What country has an estimated 72,000 emergency hospital room visits annually attributed to snow removal injuries?

What country has seen a 51% growth in college enrollments among minorities between 1993 and 2003, at the same time there was an increase of about 3% in white enrollments?

What country has 2,400,000 people pass away yearly?

What country had submariners in the Pacific with the highest fatality rate during WWII followed closely by air crews that flew bombers over Germany?

What country has one state that loses $576,000,000 yearly in unpaid cigarette taxes due to tax free sales on Indian reservations?

What country interned 110,000 people of Japanese ancestry (two-thirds whom were citizens), sometimes at gunpoint, into internment camps that were in some cases, horse stalls and tar paper shacks, during the early part of WWII?

What country still had one state that outlawed the practice of tattooing, and had actually imprisoned some who were guilty?

What country had the CEO of a company that had its stock decline almost 8% in 2005, top all other CEOs with earnings of $469,000,000?

What country's teens have a gonorrhea rate that is 70 times higher than that of their peers in the Netherlands and France?

What country has an estimated 200,000 homeless veterans, of whom about 6,000 are from the Afghan and Iraq wars, in 2006?

What country had about 25,000,000 veterans, in 2006?

What country lost 50 women in the Iraq war, up until 2006?

What country's commercial airlines have cumulatively lost over $50,000,000,000 between 2000 and 2006?

What country's passengers on a typical domestic commercial airline will pay a seat price that varies between $159 and something over $900, for the same flight?

What country had 994 black fighter pilots during WWII?

What country has a large building that houses the top echelon of senior military and civilians, and whose halls and corridors extend over 17 miles?

What country used potable water to flush toilets, while 2,600,000,000 people in the world have no decent place to even go to the bathroom, let alone good water to drink?

What country, in 2006, has no Wal-Mart in its largest city?

What country has made a hero out of Jesse James, who rode with Bloody Bill Anderson's ruthless Confederate guerrillas who were responsible for terrible atrocities during the Civil War?

What country has a CEO pay rate of 475 to 1 for the average employee, while the rate in Britain is 24 to 1, and in France is 15 to 1 and in Sweden is 13 to 1?

What country levies a fine of $250,000 plus 10 years in prison for anyone caught importing Cuban products?

What country's big 3 auto makers spend more on health insurance than on steel?

What country had 15 consecutive votes in the United Nations General Assembly against their embargo against the island of Cuba?

What country has a radio personality that is paid $1000 every working 24 seconds, while the police and school teachers are paid the same for every 43 hours they work?

What country has a Defense Department that purchases the most commercial airline tickets of anyone in the world?

What country has a grocery supermarket that uses 475,000 truck loads of products yearly?

What country has a first class airline round-trip ticket to Hong Kong priced at $11,500?

What country has a medium size city that is home to over 1500 homeless street kids, who are mostly black tar heroin users?

What country has 5,600,000 people earning just the minimum wage?

What country had a President who vetoed a highway bill in 1987 because it had 152 "earmarks" in it, but in 2005 had a President sign a transportation bill that had 6,371 "earmarks" in it?

What country had an estimated 300,000 women who received breast augmentation surgery in 2006?

What country will have a Medicare Part D yearly drug cost of over $11,000 while the Veteran's Administration is paying just over $4,000 for the same drug?

What country had the population of its Catholic nuns drop from 179,000 to just 67,000 between 1965 and 2006?

What country found that 93% of the winning candidates for the House of Representatives in 2006, spent the most money?

What country's prison inmates have a high school drop out rate of 68%?

What country has an estimated 2,500 students who drop out of high school daily?

What country has about one-third of high school students who begin their freshmen years, fail to graduate?

What country has some 39,000,000 young people from ages 25 to 34, still living with their parents?

What country was home to a religious cult that moved to Guyana where over 900 of them committed mass suicide by drinking ''Kool-Aid'' that was laced with poison?

What country offered to withdraw their missiles from Turkey and Italy in exchange for having the USSR remove its missiles from Cuba?

What country's income for the bottom 90% grew at a rate of 2% between 1990 and 2004, while the top 1% grew at a rate of 57%?

What country has five major league baseball players with contracts for $252,000,000, $189,000,000, $160,000,000, $141,000,000 and $136,000,000?

What country has a government that raised nearly $5,000,000,000 by minting a state-quarter series of coins, that have been taken out of circulation by coin collectors?

What country's latest popular cosmetic surgery consists of eyelash transplants at a cost of about $3,000 per lid?

What country discharged 742 military service members for homosexuality in 2005?

What country's pentagon has reclassified homosexuality with conditions like ''repeated VD infections,'' ''obesity,'' ''repeated bed wetting'' and ''dyslexia''?

What country has a 68-ton tank that travels at over 40 mph, uses 1 gallon of gas per mile, with a 500 gallon tank, needs 5 support trucks for every tank in the field, and can burn gasoline, kerosene, or alcohol?

What country had a company pay $400,000,000 to a major league baseball team for the right to have their new stadium named after the company for twenty years?

What country spends over $550,000,000 on internet dating annually?

What country has 1,700,000 men buying diamond rings annually?

What country invaded the island of Okinawa with some 1,400 ships and over 150,000 troops during WWII and in the end, claimed the lives of nearly a quarter of a million people?

What country has nearly 4 out of every 10 babies born out of wedlock, amounting to about 1,500,000 babies?

What country has its 85-year-and-older people, as its fastest growing segment of the population?

What country had a Speaker of the House of Representatives who had a staff of about 60 people?

What country has more than 500 times as many people dying on their roads as in airline accidents?

What country has about 600 people dying yearly from falling out of bed?

What country revised an annual report on hunger, to read that 4,400,000 people suffer from "very low food security?"

What country has paid whistle-blowers over $190,000,000?

What country had a House of Representatives that took 140 hours of sworn testimony in an attempt to get to the bottom of whether or not a president had misused the White House card list, for political purposes?

What country still has 7 states that have "alienation of affection" laws, and one recent judgment was for $2,000,000?

What country had 4,000,000 slaves in 1860?

What country has over 300,000 people having back surgery yearly?

What country has 70% of the wealthiest kids graduating from college, while just 8% of the poorest kids do the same?

What country lost perhaps 10,000 men in just one famous battle during their Civil War and 21,000 wounded?

What country has a town named "Tightwad," with 63 residents?

What country publicly apologized to, and paid a citizen $2,000,000 for "serious missteps" by the FBI in arresting and jailing him in a botched investigation pertaining to a bombing in Madrid?

What country's kids rank 24th in the world in mathematics?

What country medicates HIV-positive pregnant women to achieve a 99% rate for not transmitting the disease to their baby, while pregnant women in Africa transmitted the disease to 500,000 of their babies in 2005?

What country saw the first black football player drafted into the professional National Football League in 1949?

What country had an elderly woman lease 3 telephones over a twenty-two-year period at a cost of about $6,400, when she could have bought them for $20 each?

What country had over 147,000 deaths due to poisoning between 2001 and 2004?

What country awarded 464 Medals of Honor during WWII and just 2 over the same length of time in the war in Iraq?

What country awarded the second highest medal, the Service Cross, to 8,716 during WWII and just 26 during the same length of time in the war in Iraq?

What country's Army has presented 52,000 Bronze Stars to its personnel between 2001 and 2006, and just 1,500 for the Marines during the same period?

What country releases about 630,000 prison inmates annually?

What country has so-called destination clubs that allow members to stay in their luxury resort homes for some thirty days a year, after they pay a $1,300,000 join-up fee, and annual fees of up to $30,000?

What country has one state where over 10,000 people put themselves on its compulsive gambler's "voluntary" exclusion program that provides for strict penalties for those who visit casinos?

What country has cars that travel 15,000 miles at about 25 miles per gallon, and expel about 5.5 tons of carbon dioxide in a year?

What country has about 700 people who die from exposure and hypothermia yearly?

What country's people have fallen victim to a variety of Nigerian computer e-mail scams, involving get-rich-quick ploys, to the tune of around $750,000,000 per year?

What country in the 1940's discovered that Albert Einstein's brain was about 10% smaller than the average brain?

What country has a jumbo jet that sold for $275,000,000 in 2006?

What country has a huge company that buys mortgages, and had to restate their earnings by $6,300,000,000 in 2006?

What country had 95 people meeting their death in attempts to climb its highest mountain?

What country has one large city that has more miles of roads than the entire state of Alaska?

What country has major companies that spend millions of dollars for advertising, telling potential customers not to buy their product?

What country had an inmate escape from a prison and run off with the deputy warden's wife, onto to be found some 11 years later living with the woman, and her claiming that she had been held against her will?

What country has 12,000 babies born yearly, with hearing loss?

What country had an estimated $231,000,000,000 trade deficit with China in 2006?

What country dropped more bombs in Viet Nam than all of the bombs dropped during WWII by all sides?

What country has a rule banning citizens from about 20 countries from working on Pentagon contracts, awarded to countries including Canada?

What country has over 75,000,000 people who fall sick yearly due to contaminated food?

What country regularly prescribes 189,000,000 prescriptions for anti-depression drugs, yearly?

What country has 38,000,000 people eligible for food stamps, but just 60% receive them, and just 28% of the eligible elderly?

What country has provided some $93,000,000,000 in farm subsidies between 2002 and 2006, with 70% going to just 10% of the recipients?

What country's Interior Department mismanaged its responsibility so poorly that up to an estimated $10,000,000,000 in taxes was avoided by energy companies who extracted oil and natural gas from federal waters?

What country learned that a study determined that the bottom 1/2 of the world's adult population must make do with just 1% of global wealth?

What country experienced over 785,000 in job layoffs during 2006?

What country has China owning $339,000,000,000 in its Treasury bills?

What country has 12,000 homeless people "living" in a large city's downtown area, and has some 90,000 transients in its entire surrounding county?

What country has one state that has over 173,000 prison inmates yearly, at a cost to taxpayers of $8,000,000,000?

What country had over 100,000 civilians in Iraq on government contracts, in 2006?

What country has over 100 infant deaths yearly due to them being left in cars by parents?

What country's people buy over 2,100,000,000 pairs of imported shoes every year?

What country has about 3,500,000 homeless people at any given time of the year, with 200,000 being veterans, and one-third are families with children?

What country had 1,400,000 users of meth during 2006?

What country had someone who paid $450,000 for the two flags that were mounted on the car President Kennedy was in when shot?

What country had a major league baseball team that paid over $50,000,000 for the "right to negotiate" with a baseball pitcher from Japan?

What country has seen the average cost to fly commercially go from 25¢ a mile in 1978, to 12¢ a mile in 2005, in dollars adjusted for inflation?

What country makes pennies that cost 1.73¢ each, and nickels that cost 8.74¢ in 2006?

What country has 5% of the world's population, but consumes 25% of the world's oil supply?

What country purchases over one half of the world's diamonds?

What country has 80,000,000 acres of national parks?

What country has 6 states that make it a crime for a couple of opposite sex to live together as man and wife, if they are unmarried?

What country saw Wall Street handing out $24,000,000,000 in bonuses at the end of 2006?

What country has marijuana as its top selling agriculture product, at an estimated $36,000,000,000 yearly?

What country is the only developed country in the world that taxes its citizens while they live overseas?

What country spent $160,000,000,000 on alcoholic beverages in 2005, up almost 50% from 1995?

What country had one small southern state that had 10,000 children in state care in 2004?

What country charged 37 of its military servicemen with murder during the first four years of the Iraq war?

What country had one Wall Street trading company in 2006 with 26,467 employees, who were paid $16,500,000,000 for an average pay of over $623,000 each?

What country had 19,800 life insurance policy holders who stopped paying their premiums in 2006?

What country had 151,000 job cuts in the auto industry during 2006?

What country had 1.6% women CEOs of the Fortune 500 companies, in 2005?

What country sentenced a seventeen-year-old black boy and honor student, to 10 years in prison with no chance of parole, for having received consensual oral sex from a 15 year old girl?

What country has an internet company that received over 4,000,000 orders in one business day?

What country had the first woman run for its House of Representatives in 1866, and received twenty-four votes?

What country has about 7,000,000 prison inmates, or people on parole, or probation, at any one time?

What country had a major drug company who gave a departing CEO a severance package of $200,000,000 despite the fact that $137,000,000,000 of the company's market value vaporized during his watch?

What country has 39 states that still permit so-called "Payday" loans of two weeks to individuals that carry up to a 520% annual rate of interest?

What country's lawmakers refused to raise the federal minimum wage for low income workers, for about a decade, while the cost of living was going up 26%, and they raised their own salaries nine times?

What country had 1,440,000,000 people who purchased movie theater tickets during 2006?

What country has a minimum wage that was about half as much as Britain's in 2006?

What country has seen the number of diabetics swell some 80% between the years 1996 and 2006?

What country has an estimated 1,200,000 cars stolen annually?

What country has twenty-six states that have laws that allow people over age 70 to be excused from jury duty?

What country has about 2,400,000 grandparents who are raising young children?

What country has about 15,000,000 adult children who are taking care of their aging parents?

What country has people who have saved over 129,000,000 Elvis Presley 29¢ postage stamps issued in 1993?

What country will be paying a congressman who was convicted of a felony while in office, and is in prison, a pension of $64,000 per year for life?

What country has food-borne microbes that make some 76,000,000 people sick per year with 325,000 ending up in the hospital?

What country has a law that prevents its own coastal shippers from buying ships made in other countries?

What country has a Navy that has a total tonnage that equals the combined tonnage of the next largest navies in 17 countries?

What country has its largest state, with the smallest prison population?

What country pays a professional football coach $8,000,000 per year?

What country has one city that had 28 attacks on so-called "meter maids" in 2006?

What country had nearly 20,000 Marines stationed on Okinawa some 50 years after the end of WWII?

What country has over 200,000 kids kidnapped yearly by family members and another almost 60,000 by non-family members?

What country has an IRS that expects to turn over some 446,000 tax cases to private debt collectors by 2009, where they will receive 25¢ of whatever they collect?

What country found that of some $80,000,000,000 spent on gift cards in 2006, about $8,000,000,000 will never be redeemed?

What country has about 800,000 children reported missing yearly?

What country has one gambling casino that has about 1,500 cameras viewing the action?

What country has over 3,000,000 obese pet dogs?

What country had a professional football player retire, and immediately sign a TV contract for five years totaling $75,000,000?

What country had a recent survey of Roman Catholic dioceses disclose that 85% of them admitted that church money had been embezzled in the past five years?

What country had a former president pass away who, after his death, allowed his opinions of other presidents to be made public, including Jimmy Carter as a "disaster," Ronald Reagan as "receiving too much credit for ending the cold war," Jack Kennedy as "overrated," Bill Clinton as "average," and Nixon as a foreign policy "master"?

What country has 5,500,000 college students who receive subsidized student loans yearly?

What country has about 90,000,000 cats and over 73,000,000 dogs?

What country has about 29,000,000 people who spent at least one overnight trip with a pet in 2006 . . . an increase of almost 100% over 2003?

What country had over 200 companies investigated for backdating stock options that would give their executives financial windfalls?

What country has some 2,000,000 patients who get a hospital-acquired infection annually?

What country has almost $15,000,000,000 levied on credit card holders in late and over-limit penalties yearly?

What country processes nearly 40,000,000,000 checks yearly?

What country had its oil companies report some $36,000,000,000 in profits in 2005, while the congress at the same time was voting for $16,000,000,000 in more tax cuts for them?

What country has twice as many males killed in vehicular accidents, as females yearly?

What country had Medicare pay some $54,000,000,000 out in nursing home care for the poor in 2005?

What country had one large city where kids attended school a total of eight weeks longer than kids in another large midwest city?

What country exonerated some 232 people who had been convicted of serious crimes between 1989 and 2006, due to DNA testing?

What country has learned that just 38% of sexual assaults and rapes are reported to authorities?

What country has a death rate on motorcycles to be thirty-two times that of other vehicle accidents?

What country has a state where a person can get up to 30 days in jail and a fine of $500 for smoking in his/her own car?

What country has 85% of all pregnancies in which Down syndrome is diagnosed . . . end in abortions?

What country has 54% of its population living within 50 miles of a coastline?

What country's insurance industry cleared a profit of $65,000,000,000 in 2006 including property, life, and auto insurance?

What country had one homeowner's insurance policy increase from less than $400 in the year 2000, to over $5,000 in 2006?

What country's insurance losses related to weather go from about $1,000,000,000 in the 70s, to $17,000,000,000 in the 80s, and to $71,000,000,000 in 2005?

What country has 20,000 people in 31 "supermax" prisons confined to a cell of 7' × 14' twenty-three hours per day?

What country has scientists who have discovered that 8% of sheep are "gay"?

What country has the risk of having a baby with Down Syndrome of 1 in every 100 for those women over 40?

What country lost some 300 ships during WWII to Japanese kamikaze airplane attacks?

What country bought 1000 Luger pistols for their army from Germany in 1901, for about $25 each?

What country's WWI hero, Sergeant York, was at one time a conscientious objector against wars?

What country has a federal law that prohibits disabled workers from being covered by the federal minimum wage law?

What country is investigating a child pornography ring that has led to the identification of 600 suspects?

What country found 150 pythons in its Everglades in 2005?

What country estimated the cost to clean up the World Trade Center tragedy to be 7 billion dollars, and did it for 750 million dollars?

What country has learned that 5,200 pounds of carbon per passenger is emitted in a round-trip airline flight between New York and Tokyo?

What country has a medium-sized southern state that has 410,000 people licensed to carry concealed weapons?

What country has about 19,000,000 people caring for someone over 75?

What country had about 38,000,000 living below the federal poverty line in 2006?

What country spends over $40,000,000 buying "Girls Gone Wild" videos yearly?

What country paid the ruler of Tripoli a price of $52,000 in tribute for him to allow their ships in "his" waters?

What country pledged over $400,000,000 for tsunami aid in 2004 and by 2007 had only contributed $102,000,000?

What country pays a major league baseball pitcher over $514,000 every time he takes the mound?

What country has nearly 20,000 people dying yearly from drugs and drug overdoses?

What country has an estimated 300,000 mental patients in jails and prisons?

What country had half of their states where marriages between blacks and whites were illegal in the 1950s?

What country has 4% of the world's population, but consumes 66% of the world's illegal drugs?

What country has about 1,000 automatic federal and state protective benefits and responsibilities that married couples enjoy and that are denied to gay or lesbian couples?

What country lost 90 helicopters in the first four years of the Iraqi war?

What country had an auto company that lost $5,800,000,000 in just three months during 2005?

What country spends about $50,000,000,000 on weddings annually?

What country has 2,400,000 women over the age of 15 who are married but not living with their husbands?

What country had a president in the 40s who wrote in his diary, ''The Jews I find are very selfish, neither Hitler or Stalin has anything on them for cruelty or mistreatment to the underdog.''

What country has 13,000 of its youngsters taking their first alcoholic drink, every day?

What country had 2,000,000 households declare bankruptcy in 2006?

What country has 89,000,000 credit union members?

What country's commercial airline industry lost $35,000,000,000 between 2001 and 2005?

What country has 4 out of every 10 who are eligible for rebates, never collect them?

What country recalled 160,000,000 pieces of children's jewelry that contain lead?

What country's 19,000 Catholic parishes gather about $6,000,000,000 from congregations?

What country had an audit reveal that a Catholic priest allegedly mis-appropriated some $8,600,000 over a 42-year period, including giving a "girlfriend" $134,000 and purchasing an oceanfront condo for $455,000?

What country, at the current rate, would have one-third of all women who get pregnant, have an abortion by the time they are 45?

What country has 21,000 violent gangs with about 700,000 members?

What country has 30,000 servicemen killed or wounded in the North Atlantic during WWII?

What country had a plan to attach tiny incendiary bombs to thousands of bats, and to drop them on Japan during WWII, but the war ended before it could be put into action?

What country, over the past 50 years, has seen men kill themselves at a rate of over 4 times that of women?

What country had 6,000,000 men diagnosed with depression during 2007?

What country adds about 70 days to the life expectancy of its people, every year?

What country had an insurance industry that recorded $43,000,000,000 in profits for the year of Katrina and $60,000,000,000 for the year after Katrina, 2006?

What country has 2,800,000 charities?

What country has dollar bills that have an average life of only about 20 months?

What country has about 50,000,000 who buy a newspaper daily, and about 100,000,000 who read one?

What country has eleven states that are considering laws to allow pets and farm animals to be included in orders of protection by victims of domestic violence?

What country spent $10,000,000,000 on its Afghanistan war, $61,000,000,000 for the first Gulf War, and approaching $746,000,000,000 through 2008 in Iraq?

What country in 2007 had estimated that future disability and health benefits from the Iraqi war will approach $600,000,000,000?

What country in 2000 had a future president promise to have a "humble foreign policy," if elected?

What country had a president who said in 1988, "I will never apologize for the United States. I don't care what the facts are"?

What country has done virtually nothing to halt malaria from causing 3,000 children to die every day of the year throughout the world?

What country has one-third of those infected with HIV, ignorant of knowing it?

What country has 6 people who have their identity stolen every minute of every day?

What country, prior to the Japanese bombing of Pearl Harbor in 1941, had frozen all of Japan's assets, and placed an embargo on selling them any oil?

What country spied upon communications between Japanese negotiators and their home country during negotiations in Washington to limit shipbuilding in 1922, resulting in a most unsatisfactory treaty to many in Japan?

What country has 3 times as many black as white fetuses aborted, although blacks represent less than 20% of the population?

What country has some 22,000 "payday" loan locations that garner $6,000,000,000 annually, and paying back $1,600 for a $500 loan is not so unusual?

What country has 600,000 registered sex offenders living throughout the entire country?

What country had 5,500 illegal immigrants in prisons in one state, and a total of 18,000 in the year 2007?

What country has over 150,000,000 prescriptions written yearly for off-label purposes?

What country has an estimated 23,000,000 people who are addicted to either drugs or alcohol?

What country had a proposed military budget in 2007 of $481,000,000,000 while China has a budget of about one tenth of that?

What country still has 7 states that ban cohabitation?

What country has rich people stashing assets in offshore accounts that cost the treasury an estimated $70,000,000,000 per year in lost taxes?

What country has a state that passed a law against smoking in a vehicle where children are present?

What country has 40,000,000 people of Irish descent as residents?

What country paid many of the private civilian security guards who worked in Iraq in 2007, $160,000 per year?

What country's citizens purchased just 288 Toyotas in 1957?

What country has 750,000 gallbladder removal surgeries yearly?

What country's auto manufacturers have to add $1200 to the cost of each vehicle they produce, while Toyota just has to add about $200?

What country sprayed some 20,000,000 gallons of ''Agent Orange'' in Viet Nam to defoliate their forests, leaving behind for years, a residue of dioxin?

What country had 900,000 homes in foreclosure in the early part of 2007?

What country essentially told Saudi Arabia that $50,000,000,000 would be the cost to guarantee their safety from Iraq during the run-up to the first Gulf War, and they paid it?

What country had over 45,000,000 prescriptions for sleep aids in 2006, in addition to the millions of over-the-counter pills purchased?

What country had one state where the state troopers had fifteen of their men commit suicide over a four year period?

What country allowed asylum to 200 people from Iraq during the same period that Sweden allowed it to 9,000?

What country has from thirty to fifty so-called ''serial killers'' who are active at any given time?

What country provides automatic citizenship for an estimated 350,000 babies per year, born to illegal immigrants?

What country has over 10,400,000 paintball shooting enthusiasts?

What country has most everyone sleeping in a bed at night, while in the rest of the world, less than 25% sleep in beds at night?

What country has eye doctors that repair 3,000,000 eyes yearly that have cataracts?

What country had 400,000 fraud-related complaints reported to the FTC in 2005, compared to just 16,000 in 1996?

What country had 8,000 reverse home mortgages in 2001 for folks 62 and older, and 86,000 in 2006?

What country had 57,000 cases of forged Treasury Department checks in 2006?

What country has one state that has determined that it costs the taxpayers $42,000 per year to incarcerate someone . . . nearly a million dollars for a 20-year sentence?

What country had 30,000,000 bison in 1840, down to only 1,000 in 1890, and back up to 450,000 in 2006?

What country had 5,000,000 people with Alzheimer's disease in 2007 and is forecasted to have 16,000,0000 by the year 2050?

What country has 70% of its Alzheimer's population who are not in nursing homes?

What country has 42% of its population of those over 85, with Alzheimer's disease?

What country has an estimated 12,000,000 school children who become infected with head lice yearly?

What country has purchased over $2,000,000,000,000 worth of "As seen on TV" items?

What country has over 2,000 young children treated in hospital emergency rooms after being backed over by drivers, yearly?

What country's prescription drug use was up 40% between 2001 and 2006?

What country granted 1,300,000 people legal permanent residency in 2006, the first step towards citizenship?

What country has over 49,000 people named John Smith?

What country has 50,000,000 families that have benefited from the Medical Leave Act of 1993 that allow eligible employees to take up to twelve weeks of unpaid leave for the birth of a child, or other serious illnesses without losing their jobs?

What country has studies that show 82% of married people have kept at least one new purchase hidden from their spouse?

What country had a settlement between tobacco companies and the states that provides for $246,000,000,000 to be paid to the states over 25 years, but less than 3% of the money is being used by the states to discourage smoking?

What country ranks 139th when it comes to voter turnout in elections?

What country pays its farmers not to plant crops on 40,000,000 acres of land?

What country suspended 15 kindergartners for sexual harassment in one state in the school year 2005-2006?

What country had 6,266 bank robberies in 2005?

What country's people spend $8,000,000,000 on cosmetics annually?

What country had 10,500,000 cancer survivors in 2007?

What country will see about one-third of all their people being diagnosed with cancer at sometime in their lifetime?

What country imports $10,000,000,000 more in food than it exports?

What country supplied WWII soldiers with gear (helmet, weapon, uniform, canteen, etc.) at a cost of $175 and $1,500 for Viet Nam soldiers, and $17,000 for Baghdad soldiers (all in 2007 dollars)?

What country has over 38,000,000 members of AARP?

What country has 42% of those between 65 and 75, with assets worth $250,000 or more?

What country's Medicare, Medicaid and Social Security constitute 44% of the 2007 federal budget?

What country has over 76,000,000 food-borne illnesses annually?

What country still has 8,100 missing from the Korean War?

What country has a federal and state health insurance plan for kids under nineteen whose parents make too much money to qualify for Medicaid, but still cannot afford health insurance . . . The program was funded $5,700,000,000 for 2007.

What country consumes 1,500,000 barrels of oil per year, producing the plastic bottles that contain bottled water?

What country witnessed a heat wave in Europe the claimed 35,000 lives in 2003?

What country has spent $4,000,000,000 on advertisements and other methods, trying to get men and women to sign up for the volunteer armed services as of 2007?

What country has 50,000 law enforcement officers assaulted yearly and about sixty killed?

What country has seniors who outlive their driving ability by eight to ten years?

What country has a student loan industry that is worth $85,000,000,000?

What country has blacks making up 70% of the National Football League, but just 8% of major league baseball players?

What country had 75% of all Hollywood movies in 2007 that show tobacco use?

What country in 1925 permitted resident non-citizens to vote in local and even federal elections?

What country has 70,000,000 gun owners?

What country had on-line dating sites with an estimated revenue of $649,000,000 in 2006?

What country had 8,400,000 people who had their identity stolen, for a loss of over $49,000,000,000 in 2006?

What country's Coast Guard stopped a ship carrying 40,000 pounds of cocaine in 2007?

What country has 3,000 people waiting for heart transplants, but only a little over 2,000 available, yearly?

What country spent $1,400,000,000 in 2004 to protect 1271 threatened and endangered species?

What country learned that some 300,000 whales, porpoises and dolphins die yearly from entanglements with fishing gear?

What country has over 70,000,000 who go to theme parks in one part of the country yearly?

What country has a man who has survived over 160 poisonous snake bites over the years?

What country has an estimated 1,000 homicides per year that are committed by people suffering from mental illnesses?

What country has over 4,000,000 members of the National Rifle Association?

What country has an estimated 2,700,000 people with mental illnesses that many think should be banned from being able to buy a gun, but twenty-eight states refuse to provide mental illness data to the FBI data base?

What country has 23 states where it is illegal to sell unpasturized and unhomogonized milk for human consumption?

What country had 353 people killed in police chases in 2006, with over 100 of them innocent bystanders?

What country in 2007 has a president with a 28% favorable rating and a Vice President with 9%?

What country gave a radio talk show host a 5-year $40,000,000 contract that specified that he be "irreverent and controversial" and that he would not be fired without first getting a warning?

What country lost 4,000 soldiers while subduing a 3-year insurgency in the Philippine Islands where an estimated 500,000 Filipinos died?

What country makes 35,000,000 paper notes per day, worth some $635,000,000?

What country has over 2,000 juveniles in their prisons who have been sentenced to life without the chance of parole?

What country has one western state that has 45 juveniles in prison who have been sentenced to life without parole, while the entire rest of the world has just 12?

What country has a company with over $35,000,000,000 in yearly sales with a CEO who is a woman, and an immigrant from India?

What country had its teens dropping out of school at a rate of 6,000 per day in 2007?

What country has suicide as the second leading cause of death of their college students?

What country has administrative private health costs at about 20%, while Medicare/Medicaid administrative costs are just 3%?

What country has just 13% of its private-sector employers in 2007 who offer health benefits to retirees?

What country had 44 million Hispanics, 40 million blacks, and 13 million Asians in 2007?

What country provides Pakistan with $80,000,000 monthly in foreign aid?

What country has 130,000 prisoners who are serving life sentences?

What country has 100,000 papers being fed into a plagiarism detection site that informs colleges (including Harvard) and professors of students who are cheating?

What country has become aware that 70% of those who get genital herpes, get it when it is not apparent or visible?

What country has 2,000,000 people who develop hospital-acquired infections, yearly?

What country has between 1,000,000 and 3,000,000 people who consider themselves transgender (i.e. anyone whose gender identity or expression differs from the sex of their birth)?

What country had three companies of the Fortune 500 in the year 2000 that protected transgender employees from job discrimination, increased to 125 companies in 2007?

What country has over 2,000 youngsters who are backed over by vehicles yearly, and treated in hospitals?

What country has about 2,700,000 people suffering from mental illnesses?

What country has a relatively small religion that disfellowships over 30,000 of their members yearly?

What country had 103,000 births from mothers who were between the ages of 40 and 44 in 2006?

What country allows their military to install and operate slot machines on their bases, located overseas, since the 1980s.

What country still spends $100,000,000 a year to find fallen soldiers from earlier wars?

What country has a town in Vermont where public nudity is legal and popular?

What country passed a nepotism law that forbids a president from hiring relatives?

What country's President Coolidge had to endure the humiliating speculation about a love affair between his wife and a secret service agent after they got "lost" in the woods for several hours?

What country's high school principals earned an average of $92,965 in 2006?

What country passed a law in 1882 that forbade any immigration of Chinese into the U.S. and was not repealed until 1943?

What country's federal government contributes just 9¢ of every dollar that is spent in its public schools?

What country has 1,700,000 people earning $5.15 or less in 2007 and the federal minimum wage law had not been increased for 10 years?

What country produces 5,800,000,000 tons of coal annually?

What country experienced 250,000 pounds of horse "emissions" fouling the streets of just one city in the early 1900s?

What country had 10,000 dead horses towed away in a single large city in one year of the early 1900s?

What country rated the gas efficiency 29th on the list of features that car buyers cared about when the cost of gas was $2 per gallon in the year 2000, and in 2007 when the cost of gas is approaching $4 a gallon, it rose to just 22nd place?

What country in the year 2004 found that 100 political appointees who are regulating industries . . . used to represent as lobbyists, or lawyers, those same industries?

What country's trade deficit with China went from $50,000,000,000 in 1997, to over $232,000,000,000 in 2006?

What country has federally mandated hourly wages in some states that amount to $9.01 for "guest workers," at the same time the federal minimum wage is $5.15 per hour?

What country has 35% of their population that believes the Bible is literally true?

What country in 2006 lost 4,800 to motorcycle accidents and had another 87,000 injured?

What country called up over 400,000 National Guardsmen to serve in the Iraqi war into mid-2007?

What country has carried on trade with Cuba to the amount of $1,500,000,000 between 2001 and 2007?

What country has had one state that allowed doctor-assisted suicides of 292 people by 2007, while at the same time, imprisoning a doctor for ten years, for doing the same thing in another state?

What country disposes of 3,500,000,000 wire coat hangers yearly in landfills?

What country provides retirement funds amounting to over $1,000,000 to congressmen and former congressmen who have been convicted of serious crimes, and some of these fellows collect while still in jail?

What country has witnessed their kindergarten through 12th grade go from #1 in the world, to #19 from about 1975 to 2007?

What country had a study that showed some 248,000 hospital patient deaths, over a three-year period, could have been prevented?

What country punishes anyone who buys a Cuban cigar to ten years in prison?

What country saw 670,000 airline passengers who were bumped from their flights in 2006?

What country is seeing pollen counts steadily rising and by the year 2017 people will be reaching for the Kleenex nine days earlier than in 2007?

What country has seen the pre-industrial level of CO_2 go from 280 parts per million, to 700 million in Phoenix on a bad day?

What country has the temperature in its cities about seven degrees higher than in the countryside?

What country uses 573 liters of water per person, per day versus 87 in China?

What country has discovered that over 1,000,000,000 other people in the world lack clean water?

What country has over 90,000 people waiting for organ transplants, and about one-third of them will die waiting?

What country, in 2007, has about 160,000 military personnel in Iraq, 66,000 in Germany, 50,000 in Japan, and 28,000 in Korea?

What country has an internet system that has up to 70% spam?

What country, between 2000 and 2007, has paid people $1,300,000,000 not to farm their land?

What country provides 70% of its farm subsidies to 10% of the farmers?

What country has 136 subsidized farmers with Beverly Hills addresses?

What country has over 764,000 children and adults from suffer from cerebral palsy, and every year some 8,000 babies are added to that population?

What country put a doctor in prison for 10 to 25 years for assisting a man to die who had Lou Gehrig's disease and who wanted to commit suicide?

What country has about 50,000 people entering its borders legally, daily?

What country's Goodwill has yearly sales of $1,800,000,000, mostly clothing?

What country has a pet health and accident insurance industry that sells over $230,000,000 worth of policies yearly?

What country has made gambling of some type legal in all but two states?

What country had Presidents Theodore Roosevelt, Truman, Nixon and Clinton attempt to have a universal health plan for all . . . unsuccessfully?

What country has one county where about 800 people commit suicide every year?

What country has summer camps for dogs . . . $1,200 a week?

What country ramped up its military spending by $187,000,000,000 prior to 2007, which was more than the entire defense spending of China, Russia, India and Britain, combined?

What country has 18 of the 20 best universities in the world?

What country's share of global GDP was 20% in 1980, and increased to 29% by 2007?

What country had 1,500 kids killed by caregiver neglect or abuse in 2005?

What country has a "body farm" that keeps some 188 corpses decaying on the grass, in the woods, or buried, in an effort to study what happens to the human body after it dies?

What country has begun to include diaper changing stations in male bathrooms in some large merchandise stores?

What country has some twenty-three states that have found it necessary to exempt breast feeding from their public indecency laws?

What country has discovered that a woman who breast feeds an infant, can burn about 500 calories per day?

What country, following the end of WWII, had nearly 5,000 strikes, involving almost 5,000,000 workers?

What country averaged about 18% unemployment during the 1930s?

What country has about one-third of all prisoners who are incarcerated, with serious health problems such as HIV, cancer or diabetes?

What country has 39,000,000 people who wake up every day in poverty?

What country has about 75,000 fires of suspicious origin, yearly?

What country has as the number-one cause of death of 15- to 20-year-olds car crashes?

What country has found that beginning drivers 17 years old have about one-third as many car crashes as 16-year-olds?

What country has the cost of replacing an air bag in a car at up to $3,000?

What country fined the makers of the movie *Gone with the Wind,* $5,000 for Clark Gable using the word ''damn'' in it?

What country in 1880 had 2300 beer breweries?

What country, along with Portugal, are the only two countries in the world that do not allow openly gay people in their military?

What country has about 60,000,000 people, at any one time, undergoing therapy?

What country has 49% of men defaulting on their child support payments, while just 3% default on their used car loans?

What country has one company that sells 100,000,000 Father's Day cards and 150,000,000 Mother's Day cards?

What country has about one-third of private employers who prohibit employees from sharing pay information?

What country is ranked 96th among the ''most peaceful'' nations?

What country has lost 26 Blue Angel pilots since the program's inception?

What country disposes of some 300,000,000 tires, annually?

What country has over 100 bodies that remain unburied, over a year after hurricane Katrina, about half have been identified and family members have been notified, and the other half are not yet identified?

What country gives farm subsidies to 358,000 people, many who are very wealthy, to the tune of $9,800,000,000 per year?

What country has discovered that eyewitness misidentification is the most frequent reason for wrongful criminal convictions?

What country has more suicides than homicides?

What country has about one-third of its suicides among teenagers and gay men or women?

What country has credit card companies who are encouraging customers to put up to $120,000 of a home down payment, on their credit card?

What country has an average of 2,185 kids reported missing, daily?

What country has a visa system (H2b) that would allow 66,000 non-skilled workers into the country yearly for agricultural and other similar work, but has such stringent requirements that only a few thousand are issued yearly?

What country has two-thirds of its adult population overweight, and a $43,000,000,000 diet industry?

What country has 3% of its population (9,000,000) calling themselves atheists?

What country's families went from spending 7% of their income on health, in 1987, to 20% in 2007?

What country has one sector where about 300,000 illegal immigrants were arrested in 2006?

What country had thirty-one school children in one large city, murdered during the school year of 2006?

What country's fathers owe over $100,000,000,000 in late child support payments?

What country pressed for free elections in the Palestine Gaza Strip, but when the results were known, refused to accept the win of the Hamas government?

What country has one large city where the wealthy mayor has put a private program in place that rewards certain actions of poor people, such as giving them $50 for obtaining a library card, and other financial awards for seeing a dentist, or keeping a steady job, or graduating from high school, and others?

What country has 74% of its commercial companies that do not have sprinkler systems installed?

What country printed some 9,000,000,000 bills in 2007 . . . with 95% of them used to replace worn currency?

What country has about 7 credit/debit cards for every person over the age of 15?

What country has credit card companies who market some 6,000,000,000 solicitations yearly?

What country requires its people to be 21 before legally consuming liquor, while France has the age of 16?

What country has 257 radio talk shows in 2007, of which 91% are conservative?

What country's people pay hotels some $1,700,000,000 in fees yearly, including charges such as checking in early, late check-outs, or leaving prior to their reserved dates?

What country had more than 1,000,000 high school seniors who did not graduate in 2007?

What country provides a maximum of $2,500 to families of Iraqi civilians killed by their military forces, and $100,000 to the families of their service members killed in a combat zone?

What country has a company that is successful selling aspirin tablets for about 4¢ each, while the chemically exact same aspirin sells for less than 1¢ each, right next to it on store shelves?

What country has over 9,000,000 kids without any health insurance?

What country spent about 25¢ of every dollar for food in 1929, and just about 10¢ of every dollar for food in 2007?

What country spends about $95,000,000,000 annually, treating ailments related to overeating?

What country recommended that Taiwan buy an $18,000,000,000 military package of equipment, yet Taiwan decided to buy just $300,000,000 in 2007?

What country's people contributed some $295,000,000,000 to charities in 2006?

What country had over 600 pregnant women murdered, during the 1990s?

What country has, at any one time, about 1,500,000 big trucks on the road?

What country, since the deregulation of the trucking industry, has gone from 20,000 interstate trucking firms in 1980, to 564,000 in 2006?

What country's constitution bans the election of a president and a vice-president from the same state?

What country regularly consumes some 30,000,000,000 single serve bottles of water yearly?

What country could save some 385,000,000 gallons of gas if everyone stopped driving for one day, while if that happened in China, just 40,000,000 gallons of gas would be saved?

What country loses 1 woman in childbirth for every 2,500 births, while Sweden loses just 1in 30,000?

What country has 25% of its adult population that does not know that the earth revolves around the sun, once a year?

What country, after having won the heavyweight boxing championships of the world for so many decades, finds in 2007, the four reigning champs are from Russia, Ukraine, Kazakhstan, and Uzbekistan?

What country started the race to have nuclear weapons in 1945, only to see eight countries join in, and by 2007 they have a total of some 26,000 warheads, that are equivalent to 238,748 of so-called "Hiroshima" bombs?

What country had a man shoot and kill a 9-year-old kid, for throwing rocks at his home?

What country had 400 pairs of bald eagles in 1966, and after 40 years on the endangered species list, had some 10,000 pairs?

What country has its average citizens paying about $6,000 for health care in a system that ranks 37th in the world, versus Cuba where people pay about $200 per year, and rank 39th in the world?

What country has just 9% of non-government workers, who belong to unions?

What country has health care costs as the number-one reason for bankruptcy and homelessness?

What country has lower taxes than France, but France has free college, and health care for all?

What country has 18,000 people who die yearly for no other reason than that they cannot afford health insurance?

What country is the only country of the top 25 industrialized countries that does not have a universal health-care system for its people?

What country has installed very few security cameras in its larger cities, while London boasts some 500,000 and 4,000,000 in the entire country?

What country has about 500 people killed at railroad crossings yearly?

What country suffers from over 2,000,000 burglaries annually, at an average loss of about $1,600 each?

What country learned after the end of WWII that the Germans deployed some 40,000 sailors in their submarines, and 30,000 never came back?

What country knows that some 96% of all prisoners in prison will someday be returned to the streets?

What country has about 500,000 kids living in foster homes at any one time?

What country has amusement parks with rides that have a 1 in 9,000,000 chance of being injured?

What country has about 21,000,000 people who are employed by the federal government?

What country has about 500,000 premature births, annually?

What country loses over 375 children due to drowning in swimming pools yearly?

What country has one state that has over 70% Mormons?

What country has an average wait in hospital emergency rooms of four hours?

What country has one large sea port that ships and receives over 600,000 cargos monthly?

What country has one-fourth of all their physicians doctors who have earned their medical degrees from foreign countries?

What country's people experience up to 8,000 venomous snake bites per year, but only around 20 are fatal?

What country, five years after leading forces of the Afghan war, finds Afghanistan providing 92% of the world's opiates?

What country in 1960 had a rate of births out of wedlock at about 5%, finds that rate at 37% in 2007?

What country discovered that some 69% of the major and minor league baseball players who were suspended for using performance-enhancing drugs between 2006 & 2007, were pitchers?

What country has found that Alcohol Anonymous is effective about 20% of the time?

What country has discovered that over 12,000 people try alcohol for the first time, every day, and the same is true for 8,000 who try drugs daily?

What country still has over 71,000,000 people who are users of tobacco products?

What country has just one southern state that still denies gays and lesbians the right to adopt children, under any circumstances?

What country had 65,000 adopted children living with gays or lesbians, in 2007?

What country had one of its most prestigious newspapers (the *Wall Street Journal*) reveal, in 2003, a legal memo written by administration lawyers, arguing that the President is not bound by international or federal laws prohibiting torture?

What country has seen statistics that show about one-half of the world's people live in makeshift homes in squatter settlements, and work in shadow economies?

What country has an internet auction site that has about 6,400,000 new listings every day, and a staff of 2,000 that polices their site around the clock?

What country has banned the use of lawn darts, nationwide?

What country had 39,000 consumer complaints about internet auction sites that were serious enough to merit criminal investigations in 2006?

What country had to recall 4,800,000 built in dishwashers that pose a risk of fire?

What country had over 565,000 reports of abuse of vulnerable elder senior citizens in 2006?

What country has 78,000,000 so-called baby boomers in 2007 who have passed the age of 60?

What country has some 85% of its alcoholics, who are also smokers?

What country sentenced a husband and wife to 27 months in prison for allowing their son to have a party under their supervision where alcohol was served to teens?

What country has almost 40% of its young people between the ages of about 18 and 30 who have tattoos?

What country had almost 300 of its employees of Customs and Border protection who were investigated for corruption between 2004 and 2007?

What country had over 1,500 companies that had to restate their earnings in 2006?

What country has a 1994 Supreme Court ruling that forbids stockholders from suing lawyers, accountants, and investment banks that "aid and abet" a fraud?

What country had a company pay its CEO some $700,000 in annual salary, while he was serving time in prison?

What country's citizens spend an estimated 6,400,000,000 hours working on their taxes?

What country has a home for sale that has monthly payments of over $850,0900, after a substantial down payment?

What country in 2007 was spending an estimated $10,000,000,000 per month in its war in Iraq, and over $758,000,000,000 since its inception?

What country put Frank Sinatra in jail in 1938 for adultery?

What country accepted some 140,000 refugees from Viet Nam towards the end of the conflict, and after?

What country had one large city Catholic diocese that paid over $660,000,000 to 508 people who had been sexually abused by priests?

What country had a home that sold for $120,000 in 1947, and is up for sale at a price of $165,000,000 in 2007?

What country closed about one-third of all of its beaches due to bacteria contamination in 2006?

What country's citizens are about 7,223,000,000 collective pounds overweight?

What country has 50% of its women over eighteen buying plus-size clothing?

What country has over 300,000 one-to-six-year-olds who are too heavy for most age-appropriate car seats?

What country's credit card late fees have increased 162% since 1995, to an average of $34?

What country imported some $75,000,000,000 in food products in 2006?

What country has more "escort services" than McDonald's in its capitol city?

What country spent over $5,000,000,000 on advertising medicines in 2006?

What country had about 65% of college graduates moving back home in 2007?

What country has about 250,000 people every year, whose heart stops beating while at work, on the street, or at home?

What country has some 800 people who have signed up to have their heads, or their entire body frozen in liquid nitrogen, in the hope that someday they can be thawed and restored to life?

What country has 47,000,000 sets of finger prints on record?

What country has built a new prison that cost $59,000,000 in 2004, but had not opened as of 2007 because the state would not support the cost of $20,000,000 per year to run it?

What country has a drug company that had to pay over $634,000,000 for claiming for 5 years that its painkiller drug was less addictive, than its competitor?

What country had the tallest people in the world for years, but is now in the middle of the pack and is led by Germans, Norwegians, and the Dutch?

What country had 49 women on death row in prisons in 2007?

What country has over 300,000 of their young adults, with cancer?

What country has 1,500,000 people who are allergic to peanuts, and about 600,000 of them are kids?

What country found the price of aluminum in 1852 to be twice that of gold?

What country accepted some 35,000 Somali immigrants during the 1990s?

What country has spent over $20,000,000,000 on health care for pets, including $3,000 pacemakers, and $8,000 for kidney transplants?

What country has over 500 prison and jail inmates who commit suicide every year?

What country has a large company with over $2,000,000,000 in bottled water sales yearly, admit that it uses public tap water in its bottles?

What country had a vice president who ordered military fighter aircraft to shoot down multiple commercial airliners following the 9/11 attack?

What country has cities that spend up to $500,000 per year removing gum from sidewalks and other areas?

What country experienced 25 fatal helicopter crashes in 2006?

What country has an estimated 40,000 people who are involved in illegal dog fighting, not including any spectators?

What country is dismayed that the country along its southern border continues to have legal bullfights, at a cost of some 30,000 bulls killed yearly?

What country has 4,000 new people diagnosed with diabetes, every day?

What country spends about 15% of GDP on healthcare for only some of its citizens, while France spends about 11% and covers everyone?

What country had all health insurers' overhead cost of $120,000,000,000, and some $40,000,000,000 of it was profit?

What country has argued that health care waiting periods in other countries are too long when everyone is covered, but countries like France, Belgium, Germany and Japan report no such problem at all?

What country has seen a dramatic increase in new truck drivers over age 50 in recent years?

What country has seen the growth of drinks loaded with caffeine spiral from about 4,000,000 cases per year in 2000, to over 80,000,000 cases in 2006?

What country's department of agriculture paid $400,000 in government subsidies, to the owner of a single soybean and corn farm, between 1999 and 2005?

What country has a large fast food corporation that back in 1955 had its largest soft drink soda at 7 ounces, and now has a 42-ounce soda?

What country's boys are 5 times more likely to commit suicide than are girls?

What country had a number of states in the early 1900s that passed laws allowing those presumed to have bad genes, to be sterilized by government order?

What country in the late 1700s had a common practice of robbing graves so medical students could learn anatomy from cadavers?

What country has companies that will even come out to homes to comb the lice out of children's hair?

What country has had over 2,000 cases of prosecutorial misconduct that led to charges being dismissed, convictions reversed, or sentences reduced, since 1970?

What country has a cell phone company that dropped some 1,000 customers because they "called customer service too often"?

What country has declared that 150,000 of its bridges are "structurally deficient" . . . after the catastrophic collapse of a huge bridge?

What country had some 4,000 people who needed someone to drive them or tow them over one long high bridge in 2006, due to fear?

What country has an estimated 10,000,000 people who have suffered strokes, and don't know it?

What country had a rule change that now allows the FBI to hire people who have smoked marijuana more than 15 times?

What country has about 80,000,000 dogs?

What country has their engineering and other prime college graduates starting at jobs paying $60,000 per year in 2007?

What country had an estimated 1,000,000 computer users who lost $2,100,000,000 over a two-year period, after giving away their personal information to scammers?

What country will have over one-half of all citizens over forty who will get an eye disease in their lifetime?

What country has some supermarkets that stock 24,000 items?

What country has over 2,000,000 people with food allergies of some sort?

What country had a $233,000,000,000 trade imbalance with China in 2006?

What country had almost a 20% drop in manufacturing employment between 2000 and 2006?

What country has a demand for paper bags that consumes 14,000,000 trees per year?

What country consumes some 88,000,000,000 plastic bags per year, using around 12,000,000 barrels of oil to produce them?

What country has an estimated 7,000,000 people who are thought to have obsessive compulsive disorder?

What country has a company that rents dogs for pets at $25 per day and $40 per day on weekends?

What country has 114 federal prisons that are removing religious books from their libraries if they are not on the approved list of 150 for each of 20 different religions?

What country loses about $800,000,000 yearly to check-washing fraud?

What country has about 5,000,000 dog attacks reported annually?

What country does it cost $36,000 for a knee replacement, when in Mexico the cost is $2,100?

What country does it take $86,000 for a coronary by-pass, when in South Africa it costs just $23,000?

What country has a 13% black population that accounts for almost 50% of all murder victims?

What country has some 45,000,000 people with tattoos, and about 8,000,000 of those regret having them?

What country is facing a nursing shortage in 2007, and yet has turned away nearly 150,000 qualified applicants due to a lack of teachers?

What country has 37% of its hotels/motels owned by Asians?

What country gets 80% of its toys from China?

What country failed to secure about 500,000,000 tons of bombs in Iraq, following the successful invasion?

What country has a government report that discloses that 190,000 AK-47 assault rifles and pistols are missing in Iraq, that were intended for Iraqi security forces?

What country's auto crash rate for sixteen-year-olds is three times that of seventeen-year-olds and five times that of 18-year-olds?

What country has the top three causes of college age kids' deaths . . . car accident, homicides, and suicides?

What country has two universities with over 91% rejection rates for applicants?

What country had 1,189 facial hair transplant procedures in 2006?

What country has 20% of all adults who believe in reincarnation?

What country almost doubled its dependence on imported oil between 1973 and 2006?

What country has a college with a system whereby the students carry cell phones that can be programmed to set to say, 15 minutes, to walk across the campus at night, and if they don't turn off the code at the end of the 15 minutes, the campus police begin tracking them through GPS locators and come to their aid?

What country has learned that there are over 100,000 earthquakes that are felt by people every year?

What country has 1500 kids under two years old, treated in hospitals annually for taking cold medications?

What country lost twenty college students to hazing, over a five year period?

What country's schools spend $8,000,000,000 yearly on the mentally retarded, but just one tenth of that for their gifted students?

What country is producing bulletproof backpacks for school children?

What country has over 205,000 students who studied at foreign universities in 2006?

What country had 2,800,000 youngsters who received medical treatment for a sports-related injury in 2003?

What country has 300,000 football related brain injuries, mostly concussions, yearly?

What country has just 16% females in their juvenile correctional population, but it is growing fast in 2007?

What country has 95% of its people who have had premarital sex according to a 2007 survey?

What country has some $82,000,000,000 owed in delinquent child support payments?

What country withheld a passport application by a man until he came up with $300,000 in back child support payments?

What country had a super athlete with a $130,000,000 contract, facing over a year in prison in 2007 for changes related to dogfighting?

What country has an organization that has built some 30,000 homes for the poor over a 30-year period?

What country has FCC regulators that have accepted over 2,500 trips over a ten-year period, from the folks they are supported to regulate?

What country finds the average little girl with eight Barbie Dolls?

What country "destroyed" $36,000,000 worth of ice that was never used during a catastrophic flood of a major city?

What country does not check IDs of people crossing the border into Mexico, thus allowing stolen vehicles and fugitives to cross without any hindrance?

What country had the originators of a popular web site delete 29,000 registered sex offender from their membership?

What country has 52% Protestant, 24% Catholic, 2% Mormon, 1% Jewish, and the balance "other" religions?

What country had just three players in the NFL who weighed over 300 pounds in 1976, and 570 in 2006?

What country is spending $7,500,000 for new uniforms for their 14,000 Border Patrol agents?

What country had the number of overseas visitors drop almost 20% between 2000 and 2007?

What country has about 1,900,000 amputees and a number forecasted to rise to 2,700,000 by 2020 due to diabetes and the Iraq war?

What country spends $14,000,000 per month to treat some 120,000 military veterans with hemorrhoids?

What country has 57,000,000 men and women who have to deal with balding, or thinning hair?

What country has one in every four companies report firing employees for improper e-mail use?

What country had a large oil company that was required to pay $2,200,000 to female employees after male workers circulated e-mails that were offensive to them?

What country is carrying on 73 independent investigations of fraud related to the Iraq war, including 100,000 AK-47s that are unaccounted for?

What country had a woman shotgun her minister husband to death while he was in bed sleeping, took off, and was tracked down and captured, and ended up spending 67 days in a mental health care facility as punishment?

What country has 200,000 people suffering from the most severe form of Tourette's syndrome?

What country routinely had about 450,000 knee replacements and over 200,000 hip replacements, yearly?

What country is now forecasting that in the year 2031 there will be some 3,500,000 knee replacements yearly?

What country had a wealthy woman who left $12,000,000 to her pet dog, when she died?

What country has about 700 acres of its West being subdivided, annexed, or paved over, every day?

What country has offered new recruits to its army a $20,000 bonus to those who report for duty within 30 days of signing up?

What country is number one in the world with ninety guns per 100 citizens, followed by India with just four guns per 100?

What country had 61,000,000 volunteers who dedicated some 8 billion hours of their time, in 2006?

What country experiences 50% of high school dropouts coming from just 15% of the schools?

What country had 65% of the women surveyed in 2005 admit that they colored their hair in the previous year?

What country had 20,000 kids go to the hospital for sticking things in their mouths in 2006?

What country has a major toy manufacturer that had to recall over 16,000,000 toys in one year?

What country has 140,000 companies that employ some workers where their names do not match their social security numbers?

What country has its average citizen spending up to five years of his/her life, waiting in lines?

What country pays a six-year police officer $75,000 a year to sit on a toilet in a stall of an airport bathroom, in an effort to combat homosexual activity?

What country spends nearly $5 billion dollars on Halloween supplies every year?

What country has about one-fourth of their credit card holders paying over 25% interest?

What country has credit card companies that hire arbitration firms to settle their disputes with their customers, and a survey revealed that these firms rule in favor of the company 96% of the time?

What country had a study that revealed that out of 4,000 children murdered, 3,000 had been killed by their parents or their primary caregiver?

What country's typical employee works 1,804 hours compared to 1,407 in Norway and 1,564 in France?

What country has some 3,000,000 people who suffer from celiac disease, a serious affliction creating an intolerance for wheat, rye and barley?

What country has their average twelfth graders with four major electronic devices in their bedrooms?

What country has about two-thirds of moms thinking their kids are of normal weight, but in fact about two-thirds of them are overweight or obese?

What country has a large city that spreads birdseed laced with birth control pills, intended to contain the pigeon population?

What country has its citizens' murder rate five times that of Canada?

What country has four of every ten workers who change jobs every year?

What country has an oral chemo pill that costs $300 each?

What country has some 7,500 health-related procedures that the government will pay for?

What country's average wedding creates $14\frac{1}{2}$ tons of carbon dioxide?

What country's average wedding cost is over $27,000?

What country used to have some 5,000,000,000 prairie dogs, but that population has dwindled to about 100,000,000?

What country has over 3,000,000 soft drink vending machines?

What country had a president who was away from the White House 484 days of his tenure, and another who was away just 79 days?

What country has 1 in 237 people who will be killed in auto accidents, while just 1 in 15,000,000 who will die in a commercial airline accident?

What country has less than 10% of its elementary schools that meet the standard of students spending 150 minutes per week in gym class?

What country in 2007, had 2,600,000 people behind on their house payments, and an additional 730,000 in foreclosure?

What country has 170,000,000 caffeine addicts?

What country has a company that spends $5,000,000,000 on health care yearly?

What country has 35,000,000 people over sixty-five and is forecasted to have almost 70,000,000 by the year 2030?

What country has about 500,000 immigrants who become citizens, yearly?

What country did not allow any photos of their military dead to be published during the first 21 months of WWII?

What country took the tiny island of Tarawa with 10,000 marines during WWII, but at the cost of 3,300 dead and wounded, after dropping over 4,000,000 pounds of munitions on it?

What country flew 1,000 planes with 24,000 paratroopers aboard during the first day of the WWII Normandy invasion?

What country had 5,500 ships taking 176,000 men across the English Channel on D-Day of WWII?

What country lost some 2,500 men on D-Day of WWII?

What country bombed a small town in France during WWII in an effort to dislodge Germans, but killed some 2,000 French civilians in the process?

What country had 16,500 men killed and wounded during the fight for the small island of Saipan?

What country was partly responsible for the deaths of some 19,000 French civilians while pushing the Germans out of France in WWII?

What country had some 10,000 citizen complaints of police behavior in one city over a three-year period?

What country has some 44 million Latinos?

What country's Indian gambling enterprise went from $12,000,000,000 in 2001 to $25,000,000,000 in 2006?

What country had a popular general in WWII that issued orders to the men on Bataan to ''fight to the last man,'' while he and his staff sailed off in a PT boat to the safety of Australia?

What country lost almost 11,000 men on the "Bataan Death March" and another 16,000 along with some Philippines would perish before the end of WWII?

What country dropped 586 tons of bombs on a religious abbey on the top of a mountain in Italy in an effort to dislodge the German defenders?

What country imprisoned some blacks during WWII for refusing to serve in segregated military units?

What country lost 7,000 and had an additional 36,000 wounded in the attack on Anzio in Italy during WWII?

What country has an auto company that provided medical insurance for 540,500 retirees and 180,500 employees, in 2007?

What country has a nonprofit group that takes surplus and distressed food and groceries and distributes it through food banks to 25,000,000 hungry people?

What country has a former president who is largely responsible for the building of 340,000 latrines in Ethiopia, in an effort to eliminate a disease that causes blindness?

What country's currency lost 40% of its value as it relates to the Euro, between 2001 and 2007?

What country has over 3,500,000 married couples living apart for reasons other than marital discord?

What country has one state where 75% of its prison population is there due to the use of methamphetamine?

What country had eight battleships, three light cruisers, three destroyers, and four other navy vessels sunk or badly damaged from Japan's attack on Pearl Harbor in 1941 . . . along with 164 aircraft destroyed and 2,403 men lost?

What country's Marines began accepting blacks in June, 1942?

What country has a drug industry that provided $18,400,000,000 retail value worth of free samples in 2005 in an effort to get patients on brand-name drugs as opposed to generic equivalents?

What country's pharmaceutical industry finds it cost-effective to spend some $30,000,000,000 a year promoting its latest brand name prescription drugs?

What country had 8 cardiologists, surgeons and a hospital that were sued and had to pay $442,000,000 for performing unnecessary procedures?

What country's consumers pay $17,500,000,000 in overdraft fees annually, almost half triggered by debit card transactions or ATM withdrawals?

What country in 1940 just prior to WWII, had about 174,000 men in the army, and that was less than the Romanian army?

What country was using a rifle designed in 1903 at the outbreak of WWII in 1941?

What country instituted the draft in the fall of 1940?

What country had insurance companies with a total surplus of $427,000,000,000 in 2005?

What country's economy grew at a rate of 1% while India's grew 8% and China's grew 12%, in 2007?

What country kept the blood supplies of white and black soldiers separate during WWII?

What country had nearly 50,000,000 men register for the draft during WWII with over 5,000,000 rejected for medical and even moral grounds if they gave the wrong answer to the question "Do you like girls?"

What country won the sea battle of Midway Island, but not before 35 of the first 41 torpedo planes were shot down before hitting any Japanese ships?

What country lost 25 oil tankers along the east coast to German submarines in January, 1942?

What country had 78,000 of their troops, along with some Philippines, surrender to the Japanese in April, 1942, and those that didn't perish remained imprisoned throughout most of WWII?

What country in 2007 lost about 1,000 WWII veterans daily?

What country had 750,000 troops in Italy during WWII and suffered some 312,000 casualties, including 23,000 who were killed while pushing the Nazis out of that country?

What country secreted 1,350 tons of mustard gas during WWII, in the Adriatic port of Bari, as a precautionary stockpile, and when the Germans bombed Bari, the ship carrying the gas blew up, resulting in some 600 Allied mustard gas casualties?

What country has one large city that in 1995 had issued fewer than 800 concealed weapons permits . . . rising to 29,000 permits issued in 2007?

What country experienced a drop in the price of solar electricity of 85% from 1982 to 2007?

What country never interned the thousands of people of Japanese ancestry who were living in Hawaii, like they did the ones living in California during WWII?

What country went into the internment camps where Japanese families were held during WWII, to recruit Japanese young men of military age to serve in the armed forces, while they kept their families behind barbed wire?

What country required an order from the president to allow combat footage of dead GI's killed during fighting on the island of Tarawa, during WWII, to be shown to the public in theaters?

What country had a radio talk show host who was fired for making a racist comment, with the victims ultimately receiving a reported $20,000,000 settlement from his former employer?

What country is it where it costs $43,200 for one year of attendance at Harvard University, and also $43,000 to incarcerate someone for a year in a large western state?

What country had a father of a ten-year-old boy pay $47,100 for him to play a cameo role in a movie?

What country had a commercial aircraft record over a ten-year period when there was one fatal accident in 4,500,000 flights?

What country has 9,000,000 children over six who are obese?

What country had a private security firm operating in Iraq whose federal workload went from $204,000 in 2000, to $600,000,000 in 2007?

What country had more private security personnel in Iraq in 2007 than troops?

What country went from a population of 130,000,000 in 1943, to 200,000,000 in 1967, and to over 300,000,000 in 2007?

What country had mathematicians that figured out in just 20 generations, a person can have over 1,000,000 grandparents?

What country contributes just $5,500,000 to Interpol's yearly budget, about the same amount being paid to a star soccer player?

What country contributes information to Interpol, where the records of 15,000,000 lost or stolen passports or travel documents are kept?

What country during WWII determined that 25 combat bombing missions from England to Germany would be enough for an airman to be sent home, but the average only reached 14, before they were wounded or killed in action?

What country initiated a massive bombing raid over Hamburg, Germany, during WWII, that set off a firestorm resulting in the death of some 40,000 civilians?

What country launched a single raid on Germany during WWII with 376 B-17 flying fortresses, that lost 60 of them, along with 600 airmen?

What country in May of 1943 and during WWII, accepted the surrender of the last German and Italian troops in North Africa, amounting to 250,000 prisoners?

What country's people experience over 1,000,000 heart attacks yearly?

What country has a defense department that detects some 3,000,000 unauthorized attempts by would-be intruders to access official networks on its computers . . . daily?

What country's administration formed a 9/11 commission that ultimately recommended that it allow the Geneva Convention standards requiring "humane treatment" of prisoners but was rejected by the same administration?

What country imprisoned terrorists in Guantanamo, Cuba, and despite the Supreme Court decisions, had just convicted one detainee in 6 years?

What country joined others in placing sanctions on Burma, leading to the shutdown of that country's exports, and thousands of laid-off women having to turn to the sex trade?

What country exports horse meat amounting to $26,000,000 annually?

What country had 2,000,000 wild mustangs in 1900 and in 2007 has just 28,000, with an additional 30,000 in federal corals waiting to be sold?

What country had a waitress for a restaurant chain rise to be CEO of that chain in about 15 years?

What country experienced 123 deaths of babies due to taking so-called infant cough drops and syrup before finally taking them off of the market?

What country has found the economic cost of car accidents to be about $230,000,000,000 per year?

What country has seen sleep duration go from a median of 8 hours in the 1950s, to about 7 in 2007?

What country ranks sixty-third in air quality among countries?

What country ranks twenty-second in water quality among countries?

What country has made it a felony to use a social security number that does not belong to you?

What country has found that the Democratic candidate running for president has failed to garner as much as 40% of the white male vote, for decades?

What country permits male workers in large companies to legally take up to 12 weeks off for unpaid parental leave, while some sixty-five other countries guarantee paid parental leave periods?

What country saw the number of their stay-at-home fathers triple between the years 1996 and 2006?

What country had 47% of their white males identify themselves as Democrats in 1952, while just 25% did in 2004?

What country experiences some 8,000 poisonous pit viper bites every year?

What country had a church in a southern state that regularly had people handle poisonous copperhead snakes, with just one bite in 15 years?

What country had a top-level administration financial officer who estimated at the onset of an Iraq war that the cost would be up to $200,000,000, and was let go?

What country's wildlife officials have estimated that the number of poached animals yearly matches the number of those taken legally?

What country's Red Cross oversees 14,000,000 units of stored blood?

What country has about 5,000,000 people who receive blood transfusions annually?

What country found that almost 18,000,000 of the 435,000,000 individual records in the Social Security Administration database contain ''discrepancies?''

What country's largest utility was forced to pay $5,000,000,000 in penalties and technology upgrades to reduce emissions, after an eight-year court battle?

What country had a public school board in one state that made the decision to offer birth control pills to girls as young as eleven years old?

What country had 1,100 confirmed tornadoes in 2006?

What country had a study that discovered that in one year there were 17,000 pregnancies of girls thirteen years old and younger?

What country has blacks being 12% of the general population, but 44% of their prison population?

What country has just 38% of Mormons who volunteer for their customary two-year missionary service?

What country had a magician who made $57,000,000 in the year 2005?

What country had over 8,000,000,000 acres worth of forest fires in 2007?

What country had a major city that is taking steps to open a ''safe injection'' room where addicts can shoot up heroin and other hard drugs under the supervision of nurses, while Canada is doing just that for some 700 people per day?

What country has had roughly 1,400,000 men and women deployed to Afghanistan and Iraq up until 2007?

What country throws away an estimated 96,000,000,000 pounds of food annually?

What country has estimated that the total value of the global market of illegal drugs is some $400,000,000,000?

What country arrests some 1,800,000 people annually for drugs, and about 40% of those are for marijuana?

What country has refused to implement the sort of syringe exchange program and other harm-related programs that have kept AIDs rates so low in countries like Britain, Australia, the Netherlands and others?

What country has locked up some 500,000 for drug law violations . . . more than the number of all people Western Europe locks up for everything?

What country had a popular TV evangelist who proclaimed that Israel's Prime Minister Ariel Sharon's massive stroke was ''divine punishment'' for ''dividing God's land?''

What country has about 8,000,000 adults who seek health information on-line, daily?

What country's Iraq and Afghanistan veterans diagnosed with post-traumatic stress disorder went from about 30,000 in 2006 to almost 50,000 in 2007?

What country has 750,000 names on its terrorist watch list in 2007?

What country has an organization called "No Free Lunch" made up of about 800 physicians (out of 8,000) who pledge not to receive drug sales reps?

What country has people who are diagnosed with multiple myeloma having to pay $9,000 per month for medications that will keep them alive?

What country controls some 700,000,000 acres of public land?

What country has shots of some anemia medications that cost $800 each?

What country has a yearly military budget that is over 100 times that of Iran?

What country cannot account for the disappearance of $8,000,000,000 of funds that were allocated to the Iraq war?

What country passed a law allowing its law enforcement officials to go into other countries to kidnap people who are wanted for crimes, and to bring them back for trial and punishment?

What country regularly jails people for gambling, while allowing nearly every state to have lotteries?

What country regularly puts people in prison for life for growing a tall, green plant?

What country has refused to sign an international agreement signed by nearly every other country that would discontinue the use of land mines?

What country has allowed some 45,000,000 people to have little or no access to good health care due to not having insurance?

What country regularly imprisons people for many years for smoking a cigarette that makes them feel good?

What country requires a state license for a hair dresser, but none for people to purchase pistols?

What country permits its border patrol officers to use deadly force in a situation where minor lawbreakers wield rocks?

What country regularly sends two or three police cars, with sirens wailing, to a verbal domestic dispute?

What country had a huge political effort to give tax breaks to those who leave up to $5,000,000 to their heirs . . . a tax advantage that would only apply to the top 1% of the population?

What country subsidizes the tobacco grower industry, that is known for causing hundreds of thousands of deaths?

What country used the deadly cluster bombs in the war with Iraq?

What country for decades has decried the preemptive attack on Pearl Harbor by the Japanese, only to initiate their own on Iraq?

What country dropped atomic bombs on Nagasaki and Hiroshima to end WWII, with no pretense of those cities being military targets?

What country mistakenly shot down a commercial airliner with a missile from a ship, killing some 300 people in the Middle East?

What country sponsored an attack on a tiny offshore island in an attempt to overthrow its revolutionary government?

What country pays some top athletes over $20,000,000 per year to perform, at the same time they pay many of their teachers around $35,000?

What country surrounded a religious compound and ultimately was responsible for the death by fire of 27 young children, and 40 adults?

What country had its National Guard enter a college campus and fire on protesting students, killing some and wounding others, and did not punish any of the Guardsmen?

What country had its battleship stand offshore and lob 2,000 pound shells into the large city of Beirut, in an effort to kill Arab guerrillas?

What country launched a missile attack upon a suspected chemical plant in a Middle East country, only to find out later that it was not a chemical plant?

What country has many of its people thinking that it's better to be guilty of a crime and wealthy, than to be innocent and poor?

What country assembled a force of some 80 SWAT and other police officers outside of a school where shots were being fired inside, and yet did not enter the building for nearly 4 hours?

What country requires subjects like geometry for graduation of its high school students, but requires no such courses in marriage and parenting?

What country's citizens spend an estimated $57,000,000,000 on illegal drugs yearly?

What country has some 130,000 women who get breast implants, yearly?

What country has an estimated 70,000,000 of its citizens who have used marijuana?

What country comes in 37th place, right behind Costa Rica, in the category of overall fairness and quality of its health care?

What country is experiencing quite a few circumstances where female high school teachers are having sex with their young male students and being prosecuted for it?

What country had a former congressman who accepted $12,000,000 from Turkey to lobby against a bill that would have declared Turkey to have committed genocide against 1,500,000 Armenians in the early 1900s?

What country imprisoned for ten years a seventeen-year-old boy for allowing a sixteen-year-old girl to perform oral sex on him, and had to wait for the state supreme court to free him in 2007?

What country discovered that smokers spend some $16,000 more on medical expenses over their lifetime, than non smokers?

What country has 23% of their children living below the poverty level, while Sweden has just over 2%?

What country devotes over $35,000,000,000 yearly to maintain its arsenal of nuclear weapons that are equivalent to 100,000 Hiroshima-type bombs?

What country launched an air strike on Libya that killed women and children because it suspected that that country might be guilty of international terrorism?

What country invaded Okinawa during WWII, and drove the Japanese out, only to militarily stay there for the next sixty-plus years?

What country would impose an embargo against an offshore island, that prohibits shipments of food and medicine to that tiny country, and keeps it in effect for over 50 years?

What country launched a military attack against a tiny island country because it was building an airstrip that it felt was threatening?

What country regularly exerts pressure on other countries that might be involved in a conflict, yet when it is their conflict, refuses to listen to any country that tries to broker a peaceful solution, nor will they talk to the country they are in disagreement with?

What country has some 240,000,000 guns in civilian hands . . . mostly handguns that are of little use for hunting?

What country has some 400 firms that charge around $100,000 for predicting how potential jurors will vote in a criminal trial, and they claim to be 96% successful?

What country has about 60% of all inmates in federal prisons there for drug offenses?

What country has over 500,000 kids living in foster homes?

What country has four times the murder rate per capita as Britain?

What country has convicted over sixty people of serious crimes and sent them to prison, only to later have DNA tests prove that they were innocent?

What country allowed a man who admitted to murdering nineteen people to go free after a brief prison sentence, because he agreed to testify against a high-ranking gangster?

What country has over 20,000 people murdered annually?

What country suffered over 55,000 of their soldiers killed, in a war that claimed some 3,000,000 people only to withdraw with no resolution many years later?

What country has three-quarters of all of the world's serial killers?

What country would commit to going to war, when their senate voted just fifty-one to forty-nine in favor of it?

What country has just about 4% of the world's population, but 25% of the world's prison population?

What country commits hundreds of billions of dollars to make war on countries like Grenada, Panama, Viet Nam or Iraq, but just 5 million dollars in aid to India after a catastrophic earthquake that killed some 50,000?

What country has over 300,000 mentally ill people in its prisons?

What country has about 4,000 cars stolen daily, and arrests only about 15% of the thieves?

What country had just about 1,000,000 people in prison in 1988, and about 2,000,000 10 years later?

What country has nearly 4,000,000 homes burglarized every year?

What country has about 5,000,000 hardcore drug addicts, and some 52,000 deaths attributed to overdoses yearly?

What country has over 1,400,000 people declaring bankruptcy yearly?

What country spends an estimated $30,000,000,000 spying on other countries during peacetime?

What countries refuses to sign the anti-land mine treaty despite the fact that there are some 300,000 land mine survivors with limbs missing who are mostly civilians?

What country had 30,000 drug arrests in 1960, and over 1,000,000 in 1990?

What country has over 1,000,000 divorces yearly?

What country has more than 50,000 children reported missing, yearly?

What country has over 6,000,000 kids taking the drug Ritalin?

What country had over 750,000 people killed or injured in the year 2000 from medication errors and adverse drug events, in hospitals?

What country gave out over 6,000,000 medals to the 500,000 service men and women who participated in the ''Desert Storm'' war?

What country has a teen pregnancy rate that is 10 times that of most other countries, and a teen AIDs rate that is about five times that of other countries?

What country has some 4,000,000 people with Alzheimer's disease, and predictions are that there will be 14,000,000 by 2050?

What country's army was rated number 16 in the world in the late 1930s, just behind Greece and Portugal?

What country allowed Hirohito to rule Japan for 45 years following their surrender after WWII, despite all of the terrible atrocities perpetrated by the Japanese during the war?

What country sent over 16,000,000 young men to war in the 1940s, and lost over 460,000 of them, with many more millions wounded?

What country had 1,100 men and women graduate from Harvard in one year, and only 12 of them ever were drafted, or served in Viet Nam?

What country entered WWII in late 1941, and saw an estimated 50,000,000 men and women and civilians killed, from all countries?

What country had nearly half of its homes without running water, private baths, and flush toilets, in 1940?

What country had 25% of their homes without electricity in 1940?

What country later paid $20,000 to each Japanese family that was "interred" in concentration camps during WWII?

What country had one divorce in six marriages in 1940, and one in two by the year 1990?

What country has 4,000,000 dog attacks on humans, mostly children, yearly?

What country has twice as many deaths due to suicides yearly, as those from AIDs?

What country joins such countries as China, Iraq, Iran, Pakistan, and Saudi Arabia when it comes to having the death penalty?

What country ended up spending over $20,000,000 defending and trying the accused bomber-killer of 158 people who were in the Oklahoma Federal Building?

What country had black legislators in Georgia vote against a bill that would give Hispanics the same business tax breaks that were already given to blacks?

What country had 10,000,000 foreign born people living in it in the year 1960, was almost 30,000,000 in the year 2000?

What country has estimated that the average cost to raise a child is over $230,000?

What country has a murder rate that is 6 times that of Japan?

What country spends over $20,000,000,000 per year treating tobacco-related illnesses?

What country has over 98,000 people reported missing yearly?

What country has over 19,000,000 people suffering from depression?

What country has more than 1,000,000 auto thefts per year?

What country took 6,000 guns away from school kids in schools in 1997?

What country had over 20,000 men who came back from Viet Nam permanently paralyzed?

What country had an estimated 10,000 Viet Nam veterans commit suicide after returning from the war?

What country offered Puerto Ricans $50,000,000 if they would vote for a continuance of its Navy being allowed to bomb a stretch of their beaches in training exercises?

What country offered hundreds of millions of dollars to Serbia, if they would turn over their former leader, Milosevic, to stand trial for war crimes?

What country permitted a defense lawyer two-and-a-half years to prepare his defense for an accused serial killer of twelve people in a western state?

What country had a president that declared that he was going to war in the early 1990s no matter how a senate vote turned out?

What country has some 13,000,000 vehicle accidents yearly?

What country had 2,641 bank robberies in a large city, in just one year?

What country has 8,000,000 of its citizens buying guns, yearly?

What country has a state that allows 200,000 people to carry a concealed weapon legally?

What country mints about one-third of all of the world's coins?

What country has over 16,000,000 people suffering from diabetes?

What country has 350,000 cases of noncustodial parents kidnapping their kids every year?

What country has about 2,100 children reported missing every day?

What country has 30,000,000 of its citizens hospitalized every year?

What country kills over 12,000,000 cats and dogs every year because they cannot find homes for them?

What country has the average wedding for well-off people costing about $80,000?

What country has over 7,000,000 kids flying on commercial airlines alone, every year . . . many are from divorced parents flying to the other parent?

What country has over 17,000 teen-age girls having face and/or body cosmetic plastic surgery, yearly?

What country has over 107,000,000 overweight people, with the majority of them being actually obese?

What country had forest fires that destroyed over 8,000,000 acres in the year 2000?

What country has 3,000,000 youngsters who have "attention deficit disorders"?

What country has committed its armed forces into military action against other countries over 125 times, and only secured a declaration of war from their congress just 5 times?

What country launched over 60 Tomahawk cruise missiles into the country of Afghanistan in an attempt to kill a suspected terrorist?

What country launched cruise missiles into Sudan in an effort to destroy a suspected germ warfare factory, only to find out later that it was a legitimate pharmaceutical factory making medicines?

What country loses 420,000 of its people yearly to premature death due to tobacco-related illnesses?

What country during WWII had 33% of its service men volunteer, leaving the other 67% to be drafted, to defend the country?

What country fought the Mexicans at the Alamo in Texas partly because Mexico did not allow slavery, and the Texans wanted the right to have slaves?

What country gave the British fifty naval destroyers to be used to defend against the German submarines, prior to its entry into WWII?

What country lost 836 merchant ships during WWII, mostly to German U-boats?

What country prints over 100,000,000 copies of the Bible every year?

What country lost 3,506 men in submarines during WWII?

What country lost 4,750 B-17 bombers and their crews to enemy action during WWII?

What country releases over 600,000 men and women from their prisons every year?

What country landed its armed forces in Algeria during WWII and had to fight the French there?

What country has over 4,600,000 people loose in the population at any one time who are either on parole or probation?

What country has about two-thirds of its currency being held in foreign countries?

What country arrested 4,000 counterfeiters during the year 1999?

What country has over 500,000 police pursuits yearly?

What country's congress passed a resolution on the Gulf of Tonkin that essentially authorized the president to pursue the Viet Nam war, only to find out years later that there never was a torpedo attack on their ships in the Gulf of Tonkin?

What country captured over 400,000 Germans during WWII, including forty generals, and brought them back across the ocean as prisoners of war to be spread out in 500 prison camps?

What country did not release their German POWs until a year and a half after WWII was over?

What country had 90,000 of their own troops being held as POWs in Europe during WWII?

What country scrambled to get German scientists at the end of WWII, not to punish them, but to treat them like royalty in order to have them work on missile projects?

What country has 50,000 of its citizens suffering from serious burns yearly?

What country has over 200,000 miles of railroad tracks?

What country had 286 West Point cadets decide to serve the Confederacy at the outbreak of the Civil War?

What country experiences over 3,000,000 battered women, yearly?

What country records over 350,000 violent acts by teens under the age of 18, every year?

What country has from thirty-five to fifty serial killers on the loose at any one time?

What country makes and consumes over 4,200,000,000 pizzas per year?

What country has over 16,000 vehicle traffic deaths caused by alcohol every year?

What country amassed 900 warships in its attack on the tiny island of Iwo Jima during WWII?

What country made forced landings of 3 B-29's in Russia during WWII, after bombing Japan, and those aircraft were reverse-engineered by the Russians who ultimately made 850 similar bombers?

What country dropped more bombs on Laos during the Viet Nam War than were dropped on Germany during the entire duration of WWII?

What country spends 9 times more on its military than the next 9 countries combined?

What country "retires" about 11,000,000 autos to junk yards, per year?

What country has about 2,000,000 miles of paved roadways, and another 2,000,000 miles of unpaved roads?

What country had a ship named the USS Liberty that was attacked by Israeli airplanes and torpedo boats while it was in international waters in 1967, killing 29 sailors and wounding 170?

What country lost 8,000 men in just one battle with the Germans during WWII, for Bastogne, France?

What country has 12,000,000 who qualify for food stamps, but do not get them?

What country lost over 9,000 men on Omaha Beach during the invasion of Normandy in WWII?

What country issued a statement of "deep regret" over the massacre of Sioux Indians at Wounded Knee, over 100 years later?

What country has over 2,000,000 women committing violent crimes every year?

What country has over 100,000,000 emergency calls to 911, yearly?

What country has over 20,000,000 of its people who own three or more cars?

What country's armed forces killed over 192,000 Japanese and took over 72,000 prisoners in the retaking of the Philippine Islands during WWII?

What country had some 30,000 men of Japanese descent serving in the military during WWII, at the same time most Japanese civilians were confined in "internment camps?"

What country's citizens have an average of over $8,000 debt per credit card?

What country has over 10,000,000 of its people collecting disability payments from the government?

What country lost 16,000 servicemen killed and over 60,000 wounded in the "Battle of the Bulge" against the Germans, towards the end of WWII?

What country experiences over 300,000 deaths per year related to obesity?

What country has arrested over 8,000,000 of its people since 1982 for smoking marijuana?

What country has about 16,000,000 people who use illegal drugs on a regular basis?

What country has one individual citizen who owns 200,000,000 acres of land?

What country had over 4,500,000 of its women join the work force during WWII who had never worked outside the home before?

What country lost 28 of its 30 "floating" 35-ton Sherman tanks, in the water, never making it to the beach, during the invasion of Normandy in WWII?

What country harvests 40,000,000 tons of salt every year, and uses just 4% in food?

What country's people burn 700 less calories per day in 2002 than they did in 1960 . . . solely due to the lack of physical activity?

What country has over 1,000,000 firefighters and about 750,000 of them are volunteers?

What country has over 2,500,000 serious crimes committed, yearly?

What country paid CEOs about 40 times what a man on a machine would make in the past, and that figure in 2006 is about 500 times?

What country buried over 9,000 men a few hundred yards from Omaha Beach, in France?

What country has, on a relative basis, fewer students graduating with PhDs than Finland?

What country had one-third of all high school students in a large western state who failed to graduate from high school in 2006?

What country has 77% of its people who think abortion should be legal?

What country had a president who spoke famously of curbing the size and influence of the federal government, but between 1981 and 1989 the size of the federal payroll grew by 40% and 200,000 people?

What country in 1992 had a third-party candidate for president who got almost 19% of the total vote?

What country worries more about breast cancer, but finds that cardiovascular diseases kill almost twice as many women as all cancers put together?

What country found that nearly two-thirds of women say they get a good night's sleep just a few nights a week?

What country's women suffer about twice as much from severe depression than men during their lifetime?

What country has 6,000,000 people who suffer from fibromyalgia, a disease that results in pain everywhere and insomnia?

What country is now recommending that eleven- and twelve-year-old girls get vaccinated against a sexually transmitted disease that infects some 80% of women, and the government will pick up the cost of $360 for 3 injections for uninsured girls?

What country has some 2,400,000 breast cancer survivors?

What country has the highest ever total of retirement funds at the end of 2006 at $16,800,000,000,000?

What country has 12% of women over 65 at the poverty level, compared to just 6% of men?

What country has implanted some 268,000 cardioverter-defibrillators in people who need it to shock their heart back to normal if it begins beating erratically?

What country now has nearly a dozen states where students can opt out of dissecting frogs?

What country in the early 1900s allowed the different state legislatures to choose who would be their federal senators?

What country has 131 sites of potentially dangerous radioactive waste material from nuclear energy plants, scattered throughout the country?

What country had more soldiers die in its civil war than in any other war in its history?

What country's people planted over 20,000,000 "victory" gardens of vegetables during WWII?

What country had just 8,000,000 auto owners during WWII and imposed gas rationing?

What country has over 12,000,000 children living below the poverty line?

What country arrested over 750,000 of its people in 2000 for smoking pot?

What country's major league baseball players make an average of over $2,800,000 per year?

What country gives first time drug offenders an average of 5 years in prison, and first time violent offenders just 4 years in prison?

What country finds the average murderer serving just 6 years in prison and the average rapist serving just 5?

What country allows its ex-cons that were convicted of murder or rape to collect welfare, food stamps, and other federal assistance once they're out of prison, but denies those benefits for the rest of the life of an ex-con who was convicted of a drug offense?

What country has more lawyers (800,000) than all of the other countries in the world, combined?

What country has over 70,000,000 computers in its landfills already, and will have over 500,000,000 in the next 5 years?

What country arrests over 2,500,000 of its children every year?

What country cut back on IRS audits of people making over 100,000 per year in 2001, and increased audits for lower income working folks by nearly one-half?

What country has 2000 women per year killed by their partners or exes?

What country has the top 10%, income-wise, who make 40% of all political contributions?

What country in 1982 had the ten highest paid executives making an average of $3.5 million, and 20 years later, that average is $155 million per year?

What country voted against the worldwide effort to cease production of, and eliminate the estimated 60,000,000 land mines that continue to kill and maim innocent civilians around the world?

What country had over 1,500,000 personal and business bankruptcies in a twelve-month period between 2001 and 2002?

What country had 100 kids killed by strangers who took them, in 2001?

What country discards over 260,000,000 auto and truck tires yearly?

What country has 10,000 of its citizens treated for amusement park accidents every year?

What country still has about 37,000 troops in South Korea, over 50 years after they were sent there at the outbreak of the war?

What country has over 20,000,000 people suffering from clinical depression?

What country invaded Mexico in 1916 with 10,000 troops in a ten-month unsuccessful effort to capture Poncho Villa?

What country has a player who signed a contract for over $250,000,000 while many school teachers are being paid over $250,000 for the same ten-year period?

What country left over 8,000 Eurasian infants behind in Viet Nam, after the war ended, and then resisted efforts by the UN to have them brought to the country their soldier-fathers lived in?

What country had a CEO of a large company who made over $100,000,000 during the same time his company's stock fell from $60 to around $2?

What country admitted, after 50 years, that their soldiers killed 82 civilians (twenty-nine of them were under ten years old) in the village of No Gun Ri, South Korea, during the opening days of the Korean conflict?

What country had over 64,000 federal employees who were rated unfit for employment, and yet just about 400 are fired every year?

What country has its courts approving "confidentiality agreements" for lawsuits whereby the public never learns how dangerous things like those Firestone tires were?

What country has over 10,000 youngsters dying from alcohol-related incidents yearly?

What country lost over 6,000 soldiers in the one day battle of Antietam, during its civil war?

What country flew over 250,000 sorties over Iraq during the 1990s, and bombed and strafed antiaircraft installations that threatened them?

What country fought the Japanese in house to house combat in Manila, the capitol of the Philippines, resulting in over 100,000 civilians being killed in 1945?

What country used 24,000 flame throwers in its war against Japan?

What country has over 40,000 colonels in its army?

What country has over 440,000 of its high school students attempt suicide yearly?

What country eradicated over 4,000,000 bison in the 1870s in an effort to subjugate the plains Indians?

What country is awarding 170,000 more college bachelor degrees yearly to women as opposed to men?

What country declared war on Spain after an explosion sunk the battleship "Maine" in a Cuban harbor, only to realize much later in 1974 that the explosion was an accident?

What country claimed the prizes of Guam, the Philippine Islands, and Guantanamo Bay after the war with Spain?

What country still has some 8,100 soldiers missing in action from the Korean conflict?

What country's servicemen drank over 10,000,000,000 Cokes during WWII?

What country had over 11,000,000 women over the age of 15 that have chosen to be permanently sterilized?

What country has over 6,000 unsolved murders every year?

What country records over 64,000 assaults per year against law enforcement officers?

What country saved Kuwait from a foreign invasion in 1991, only to find ten years later that 70% of the people of Kuwait have an unfavorable opinion of them?

What country has over 1700 women police officers in one large city?

What country supplied pilots to the Flying Tigers, who helped China defend itself against the Japanese in the early years of WWII, and shot down 296 Japanese planes in air to air combat, and only lost 4 P-40 fighters, themselves?

What country has about 10% of its land paved over with roads?

What country in the early 1960s had nuclear missiles in Turkey, poised to be launched into the USSR, at the same time they demanded that the missiles supplied to Cuba by the USSR be dismantled?

What country had some 1800 WWII veterans pass away daily, in 2002?

What country had twenty-one of its soldiers refuse to come home when POWs were released after the Korean conflict, and chose to stay in China?

What country had politicians spend over $900,000,000 in advertising and TV fees in efforts to get elected, in an off-year election?

What county deployed over 12,000 helicopters during the Viet Nam War, and lost almost 6,000 of them?

What country had some citizens pay the psychic named Miss Cleo over $500,000,000 for advice, and then sued her to get it all back?

What country has the odds of children of unmarried couples twenty-two times that of children of married couples, of going to prison?

What country contributes $1 for humanitarian foreign aid for every $17 Norway contributes?

What country contributes one-tenth of one percent of its GNP to humanitarian foreign aid?

What country lost almost 1,300 ships to German U-boats during WWII?

What country loses over $10,000,000,000 to shoplifters, yearly?

What country had over 500,000 computers and laptops stolen in 2001?

What country put women to death in the 1600s for practicing "witchcraft?"

What country was ranked 10th militarily in the 1930s behind Belgium and Greece?

What country has some 267,000 people dying from heart attacks yearly?

What country has its citizens spending over $60,000,000,000 a year on gambling?

What country has about 500,000 deserted and dangerous mine shafts scattered throughout the country?

What country has a vehicle stolen every 20 seconds of the day?

What country allows men on death row to get heart transplants?

What country passed a law in one city that prohibits young people from wearing baggy pants that droop below the hips with a penalty of up to six months in jail?

What country ranks number 41 out of 171 countries when it comes to women who die from complications of pregnancy or childbirth?

What country allowed the sterilization of mental patients in one state during the 1960s and 1970s?

What country had a CEO who earned $795,000,000 the year before the company declared bankruptcy?

What country's leaders have told their people to hate the governments or the people of the following countries over the past 50 years, only to befriend many of them decades later? . . . Germany, Italy, Turkey, North Viet Nam, Iran, Cuba, China, Panama, Bosnia, Libya, Yemen, Iraq, Syria, North Korea, Russia, Venezuela, Japan, and Afghanistan.

What country's CIA supplied Afghans with hundreds of Sidewinder missiles at no cost during their conflict with the USSR, only to attempt to buy them back years later when it began to look like they may be used against them?

What country had a backlog of over 15,000 law suits brought by prison inmates who are suing from their jail cells?

What country drafted some 34,000,000 people during WWII?

What country has over 500,000 of its people experiencing identity theft, every year?

What country had a company that had $200,000,000 in sales to folks who actually believed that they could lose weight in their sleep after taking a pill, no matter how much food they ate?

What country had one of its own citizens open fire with an automatic weapon in Palestine, killing fifty and wounding over 100 Muslims?

What country has many laws against all forms of gambling, yet also has nearly 300 Indian casinos?

What country has a record of never voting any seated federal Senator out of office for over 70 years?

What country had tens of thousands of its people rioting in 1863 against the Civil War, and opposed to the instituted draft, with 70 killed?

What country launched an attack that lasted for five days against the Canadian city of Toronto, in the early 1800s?

What country found itself in a huge scandal stemming from hundreds of allegations of sexual abuse against young children, by Roman Catholic clerics?

What country consumes over 6,000,000,000 gallons of beer yearly?

What country absolved two soldiers of all blame in a military trial after they ran over two young Korean children in their armored vehicle?

What country permitted nearly everyone to print paper money up until 1913, and about 15,000 banks and corporations were doing it?

What country provides the most foreign aid to Israel, Egypt and Turkey?

What country in 2007 was paying individual security "contractors" in Iraq up to $33,000 per month for their services?

What country's people in the early 1900s had just a 50% chance of surviving into adulthood?

What country has children at risk trick-or-treating on Halloween due to some people putting razor blades in the candy they hand out?

What country elected a president even though he obtained some 500,000 fewer notes than the man he defeated for the presidency?

What country decided unilaterally to abrogate the antiballistic missile treaty that was made with the USSR decades previously?

What country had one city with 750 police pursuits in one year?

What country decided to outlaw the sale and consumption of beer, wine and alcohol for a thirteen-year period?

What country has 50,000,000 people who suffer from high blood pressure?

What country flew 2493 dedicated missions to find and destroy Scud missiles during the Gulf war, but was unable to confirm any kills of mobile missiles or their launchers?

What country produced over 300,000 military aircraft during WWII?

What country, in 1958, had a B-47 take off with an atomic bomb, on a training mission to England, when a crewman pulled the wrong lever, dropping the 4,000 pound bomb on a home in Savannah, Georgia . . . fortunately the bomb was not activated and no serious damage occurred, but the government paid $40,000 to repair the home?

What country surrendered almost 130,000 soldiers to the Japanese in Malaysia and Singapore during the first few months of WWII?

What country has a radio talk-show host who gives family advice to an audience of over 12,000,000 people, who hasn't spoken to her mother in twenty years?

What country has over half of all of its tens of thousands of video games depicting war and killing?

What country has over 2,000,000 members of Alcoholics Anonymous?

What country's policy is that the Kyoto accord on global warming, and the treaty on the International Criminal Court should not apply to them?

What country imposed fines and penalties on its major investment banks and stock brokerages to the tune of $1,400,000,000 for misleading many thousands of their investors by recommending stocks they knew were inferior?

What country has estimated that 60,000 gastric by-pass operations were performed in 2002?

What country experienced an outbreak of violence in the early 1940s between zoot-suited Mexican young men and white sailors in a large city, leading to the president directing that sailors be restricted to their ships?

What country suffered over 500 hits on warships by Japanese kamikaze aircraft during WWII?

What country has about 100,000 people die from alcohol abuse, yearly?

What country lost seventy-five aircraft from their aircraft carriers during a severe typhoon during WWII?

What country had an aircraft carrier's flight landing deck severely twisted and damaged during a typhoon that occurred during WWII?

What country persuaded the Olympic Committee to allow professional basketball players to play in the Olympics after suffering a defeat with their amateurs?

What country has a large state that requires released sex offenders to notify authorities of their whereabouts, but could only account for about half of the 70,000 that this law applied to?

What country had 35,000 prisoners on death row awaiting execution in 2003?

What country has a huge retail company that plans to hire an additional 800,000 employees in the next five years?

What country has a famous TV judge who commands $100,000,000 for four years of thirty-minute trials?

What country had a former general running for vice president who advocated dropping an atomic bomb on Viet Nam?

What country initiated a raid on Tokyo during WWII with 300 B-29s that dropped incendiary bombs and obliterated seventeen square miles of the city, killing more civilians than were later killed in Hiroshima?

What country has over 6,000,000 vehicle crashes every year?

What country loses some 64,000 people to the flu every year?

What country had a president that took a safari to Africa and killed 550 large animals including elephants, rhinos, lions and zebras?

What country had a president who had a reputation for having a very aggressive stance and supported early entry into WWI, had a distinct change of heart after losing a son in combat while flying behind German lines?

What country has over 30,000 suicides per year?

What country has over 11,000,000 people on antidepressant prescription drugs?

What country has over 45,000 people who have ''jumped bond'' who are found and re-arrested, yearly?

What country sends 12 fly-swatters and 12 mousetraps with every 150 soldiers it deploys to the Middle East?

What country's president offered a tax cut to help the economy in 2003 that would benefit people making less than $10,000 per year by $5, and would benefit those people making a million dollars per year by $88,873?

What country has well over 1,000,000 vehicles repossessed yearly, due to non-payment of monthly installments?

What country lost 48,000 of its own men during one battle in the Civil War?

What country slaughtered over 16,000,000 buffalo over a twelve-year period?

What country lost over 1,000 ships at sea, to the enemy, during 1942?

What country has over 37,000,000 resident Hispanics?

What country had over 3,000,000 reports of child abuse during 2002?

What country lost 87 Sherman tanks during the first few days of the WWII Normandy invasion while covering only about two miles of the French hedgerows?

What country has over 900 female police officers in one large city?

What country surveyed four of its battalions of infantry during WWII in Italy and found that they had more cases of VD than battlefield casualties?

What country had an ally that lost over 8,600 bombers over Germany during WWII from ack-ack and fighter aircraft?

What country had a full-fledged coal miners' strike in the middle of WWII and had to have the president order them back to work?

What country's GIs brought back over 70,000 British war brides after WWII ended?

What country had over 358,000 cases of gonorrhea in people age fifteen to twenty-nine during the year 2000?

What country had over 30,000 narcotics arrests in one year in one city?

What country sent a smart bomb into a bunker in Iraq during the Gulf War thinking it was an army intelligence sanctuary, only to find out later that it was a bomb shelter and 293 Iraqi women and children were killed?

What country spent over $30,000,000,000 in enforcing the "no-fly" zone over Iraq in the late 1990s?

What country's police fired on college students at the Jackson State College who were demonstrating against the Viet Nam War, killing two and wounding twelve, and creating 160 bullet holes in the dormitories, and no one was ever tried or punished for it?

What country had over 10,000 people die in train-connected accidents during the year 1917?

What country has over 4,500,000 children under the age of 18 living with their grandparents?

What country had one county that put to death over 84,000 pet dogs in just one year?

What country had over $76,000,000,000 worth of vehicles stolen during 2002?

What country has an estimated 12 to 20 million people living in it illegally?

What country, at the end of the Viet Nam War, tried to evacuate seventy-six tiny orphan babies and children, only to have the aircraft crash with the loss of all aboard?

What country has over 5,000,000 unmarried couples heading households with that figure growing yearly?

What country has over 200,000 people dying from adverse prescription drug reactions every year?

What country has over 20,000 Hispanics held in jail on any given day, waiting to be deported back to Mexico?

What country has over 37,000 people killed and injured from vehicle roll-overs every year?

What country has about 40,000 non-citizens serving in the military?

What country lost 150 aircraft in one day of fighting during the battle of Midway Island in WWII?

What country has over 100,000 people working for the IRS?

What country in 1863 experienced anti-draft riots of over 50,000 people in one large city, which were put down by troops firing into the crowds?

What country had 1670 bank robberies during 2003?

What country idolized Ted Williams despite the fact that he routinely did not run out fly balls and grounders that he hit, and was once fined $5,000 for spitting at fans?

What country had over 1,700,000 babies born out of wed-lock in 1990?

What country has a large city that experiences about twenty-five bomb threats per day?

What country has a city community that regularly evacuates 170,000 school children whenever they have a nonspecific bomb threat?

What country has children who spend an average of five hours per day watching TV, playing video games, or on computers?

What country has gone from about 66% of school children walking or taking their bikes to school, to 10% over the past ten years?

What country has just 32% of its school children taking phys ed daily?

What country in 1794 had over 5,000 moonshiners marching against taxes on distilled spirits, and 13,000 federal troops were called out to put down the so-called "Whiskey Rebellion"?

What country spends about $30,000,000 on pet products and services every year?

What country has over 60,000,000 of its people infected with genital herpes?

What country's women are responsible for buying or influencing the purchase of 85% of all goods and services, nationwide?

What country had over 300 "balloon bombs" land on its west coast during WWII that were launched by Japan, and the public was never told?

What country has an estimated 100,000 gang members who belong to the infamous Crips and Bloods gangs, scattered throughout their cities?

What country's doctors write over 100,000,000 prescriptions per year for Prozac and other anti-depression drugs?

What country's top general was against the decision to drop the atomic bomb on civilian Japanese cities, and later became president?

What country has a large city that has a bomb squad that is called out nearly 1000 times a year?

What country's armed services killed approximately 107,000 Japanese soldiers during the fight for Iwo Jima in WWII?

What country has a reported case of a child abuse every ten seconds of every day?

What country paid $180,000,000 to victims of Agent Orange use in Viet Nam?

What country convicted three of its servicemen of raping a twelve-year-old girl on Okinawa?

What country had 740 people killed by their spouses in just one year?

What country has a pornography industry that takes in over $10,000,000,000 yearly?

What country has a bounty hunter company that apprehended over 23,000 fugitives in just one year?

What country has over 500,000 police pursuits every year?

What country has more police being killed from car crashes than from bullet wounds?

What country has over 600,000 Iranians living in the largest city?

What country and its allies killed an estimated 250,000 civilians in the bombing of Berlin and other German cities during WWII?

What country's pharmaceutical industry hands out over $8,000,000,000 worth of free samples to doctors?

What country's federal postal authorities refused to deliver the magazine *Playboy*, until they were directed to by a court, in the 1950s?

What country's seniors spend an average of over $2,000 per year on prescription drugs?

What country has 60,000 reported hazard material spills yearly?

What country is planning to make from 50,000 to 100,000 shipments of spent nuclear fuel to the Nevada Yucca mountain site, beginning in 2010?

What country has 103 nuclear plants scattered across the nation?

What country has more than 250 nudist camps and resorts?

What country's police estimate that 25% of all vehicles reported stolen are a direct result of insurance fraud?

What country had a major airline go bankrupt at the same time its three top executives left the company with $35,000,000 in retirement funds?

What country has had over 2,700,000 people committed to its mental institutions involuntarily?

What country still has five different ways of executing people convicted of crimes . . . gas chamber, hanging, firing squad, electric chair and lethal injection?

What country has about 1,500 people dying every day of cancer?

What country in 1967 still had sixteen states where the marriage between a black and white person was illegal?

What country's 400 wealthiest taxpayers averaged $174,000,000 each of income in the year 2000?

What country has about 104,000,000 telemarketer phone calls placed every day?

What country has over 7,000,000 sports-related injuries every year?

What country's police can incur a cost of over $500 for each hour of helicopter time, and around $70 for each hour of squad car time?

What country has a collision between a train, car, or truck every ninety minutes?

What country has 13% of its companies that don't offer any vacations?

What country's professional NBA basketball player earns an average yearly salary of $4,500,000?

What country has over 60,000,000 handguns owned by its citizens?

What country has over 200,000,000 guns of all types owned by its citizens?

What country has a southern state that has over 48,000 children as wards of that state?

What country lost sixty bombers over Germany in one raid during WWII, with ten crew members in each plane?

What country routinely flew on a daily basis during WWII, 1000 bomber and 700 fighter raids into Germany, with a total of 10,700 air force men in the two kinds of aircraft?

What country had 185 of its Navy vessels docked at one time, on December 7, 1941, at Pearl Harbor?

What country fired over 15,000 torpedoes during WWII, sinking about 5,000,000 tons of enemy ships?

What country had a major drug company that spent over $3,000,000,000 on advertising of just one drug, increasing its usage by 50% in a year?

What country's people are losing their reputation as the world's travelers, to China, where some 37,000,000 people traveled overseas in 2007?

What country has a company that rents out bees to farmers, including one who recently rented 12,000,000 bees at a cost of $27,000 to insure a profitable pumpkin crop?

What country experiences yearly rust of its military items that cost taxpayers an estimated $10,000,000,000 or more?

What country has a state that has over 7,000 people in prison for life sentences under their "three strikes" law, and just about half are nonviolent?

What country has almost 150,000,000 phone numbers registered in the "do not call" list?

What country has an estimated 500,000 square miles of coal underground?

What country had a fifty-four mile flume for carrying timbers in the late 1890s?

What country has about 37,000 tree farms?

What country has over 9,000,000 of its people suffering from macular degeneration?

What country's airports have collected over 6,000,000 knives and scissors the first few years after the 9/11 tragedy?

What country has one county where 150 people die every day?

What country has almost 1,000,000 people in wheelchairs?

What country conducts certification tests on experienced fingerprint experts who testify at criminal trials, only to see about half of them fail the test?

What country made an amphibious assault on Normandy in WWII despite the fact that the Germans had laid 330,000 land mines in the beach area?

What country overthrew the monarchy of Hawaii in 1893?

What country had laws prohibiting men from baring their chests on public beaches until the mid 1930s?

What country spent $1,300,000,000 on the Marshall Plan to rebuild Europe following WWII?

What country made over 270,000 flights into Berlin over a period of 462 days delivering food and supplies when the USSR tried to blockade the western portion of the city?

What country's servicemen married over 100,000 Japanese women during the later 1940s?

What country was pretty much responsible for creating Japan's biggest industry (prostitution) shortly after the end of WWII?

What country had strict rules for their servicemen against fraternization with German women after WWII, while MacArthur in Japan encouraged it?

What country landed about 400,000 servicemen in Japan at the conclusion of WWII and advised them that they had to salute Japanese military officers?

What country turns away over 44,000 youngsters per year who try to enter the gambling casinos on the east coast?

What country has almost 20,000 age discrimination charges filed with the authorities yearly?

What country fined its soldiers $65 for dating German women following the end of WWII?

What country issued 8 condoms per month to its servicemen during WWII?

What country's people kill each other with guns by about 11,000 per year, while England's people kill about 70, France and Australia a few hundred?

What country and its allies suffered 17,000 casualties in Korea during the twenty days it took the president of South Korea to review and accept the truce?

What country seized over 1,000,000 kilos of marijuana during 2002?

What country has over 2,100,000 people in its jails and prisons at any one time?

What country imported Volkswagen Beetles for the first time in 1949 and they were sold for about $800 each?

What country had some 78,000 fires that were set intentionally in1997?

What country's FBI arrests some 40 firefighters every year for setting fires?

What country arrested and convicted an arson investigator, working for a large western state, who authorities believe started over 2,000 fires in a seven-year period?

What country has had over 174 arson attacks on abortion clinics since 1977?

What country has over 460 commercial casinos and another 372 Indian casinos?

What country spent some $2,000,000,000 on halloween costumes in 2007?

What country has a policy of paying some soldiers who are discharged with a mental disability, monthly support for the rest of their lives that can amount to over $700,000?

What country experienced suicide from 99 active soldiers in 2006?

What country had a study by their armed forces that revealed roughly 25% of troops on their second deployment to Iraq had signs of mental illness?

What country experienced a decline in intentionally set structure fires in 2006, to about 30,000, but they killed 305 people and cost $750,000,000 in property losses?

What country has about 58,000 abductions by noncustodial parents yearly?

What country had 237 priests in one large city accused of sexual abuse of minors?

What country has a beer bottling company in a western state that ships about 700,000 cases of beer per day?

What country eradicated 420,000 pot plants that were being cultivated in one state's federal forests in 2002?

What country had a reported 7,000,000 identity thefts in 2002?

What country has about 12,000 kids injured in go-kart accidents yearly?

What country took over the building of the Panama canal after the French had lost 20,000 workers, and completed it in 1914 with the loss of an additional 10,000 workers?

What country spends over $12,000,000,000 per year attempting to stop the flow of illegal drugs?

What country has drug companies spending over $19,000,000,000 per year promoting and advertising their prescription drugs to the public?

What country has over half of the parents who are owed child support payments will not receive any payments for an entire year?

What country produced 50,000 Sherman tanks during WWII while Germany was producing about 8,000 tanks?

What country has about 87% of their criminal bail jumpers being caught by bounty hunters and returned to jail?

What country has telemarketers responsible for about $270,000,000 in sales per year?

What country has about 30,000 people per year suffering from Lou Gehrig's disease?

What country has one company which has 461,000 retired people receiving heir retirement benefits?

What country had over 15,000 murders, 87,000 cases of child sexual abuse, and 92,000 rapes during the year 2000?

What country is using a $1,000,000 facility to incinerate and destroy some 700,000 munitions filled with deadly chemicals that were leaking?

What country tried 5,700 Japanese for war crimes and convicted 3000 of them, executing 920 following WWII?

What country installed 800 security cameras in one southern public school?

What country used over 7,000 helicopters in Viet Nam, that flew over 36,000,000 sorties and had approximately 4,900 crewmen killed in action?

What country's president vetoed the bill that began Prohibition, only to have Congress override his veto in 1919?

What country had banned the sale of alcohol spirits in over half of its states by the year 1917?

What country had forty German generals and three admirals in its POW camps along with about 375,000 other German prisoners?

What country has one state that has 500,000 of its people on home dialysis?

What country had a favorable rating of less than 50% in all countries except Israel in 2007?

What country's citizens consume about 9,000,000,000 servings of french fries per year?

What country "interned" over 10,000 Germans after the outbreak of WWII and didn't release the last of them until over two years after the war ended?

What country's FBI attempted to serve a warrant on a man, but ended up killing his dog, his young son, and his wife before capturing him, only to later have to pay him $3,100,000 awarded by the courts?

What country's ATF and FBI attempted to serve a weapons violation warrant on a man, resulting in a prolonged standoff that ultimately ended up with sixty-two women and children dying, along with twenty-nine men?

What country had 40,000,000 autos in the year 1950 and over 80,000,000 just ten years later?

What country has a crash rate for aircraft landings on aircraft carriers of a little over two for every 100,000 landings?

What country launched one immense air attack from Britain to Germany that contained 1200 bombers, with an escort of 600 fighters?

What country developed and sold 747 jumbo aircraft that have carried over 1,500,000,000 passengers over the years?

What country spends over $1,700,000,000 on the drug Viagra . . . that's about nine pills being taken every second?

What country experienced a wildcat strike and walkout during WWII by workers making the Mustang fighter aircraft that had to be put down by the military?

What country had piston engines requiring complete overhauls on aircraft and advanced in a decade or so to jet aircraft requiring engine overhauls about every 20,000 hours?

What country flies commercial jets that burn a gallon of fuel every 750 feet?

What country's women undergo over 600,000 hysterectomies per year?

What country developed the small M-14 mine made mostly of plastic and meant to maim feet and legs, only to be mimicked by the Chinese who went on to produce over 100,000,000 of them?

What country's people went from a forty-seven year life expectancy in 1903 to about seventy-seven years in 2003?

What country permitted heroin, marijuana and morphine to be sold over the counter in drug stores in the year 1903?

What country has over 80,000 of its troops in Korea and Europe about fifty years after the conflicts were ended?

What country lost over sixty-five men while working on the Hoover Dam in the 1930s?

What country had one state spending $20,000 per year per pupil and other states spending about $5,000 per year per pupil when it comes to public education?

What country has over 120,000 commercial pilots who fly about 35,000 scheduled flights on any given day?

What country's population went from an average shoe size of 4 in the early 1900s to an average shoe size of 9 in 2003?

What country had a soldier boast about how he "pumped two bullets into Uday's mouth to insure his death" after the assault on the home where Saddam Hussein's two sons and grandchild were killed?

What country has some 14% of its people who claim to have seen a UFO?

What country has a medium net worth of $62,000 for someone who grew up as an only child, and just $6,000 for someone who grew up with six or more siblings?

What country had 368,000 soldiers stationed overseas in 120 countries, in the year 2003?

What country supplied hundreds of Stinger missiles, capable of shooting down aircraft, to the Afghans who were fighting the Russians, only to find them years later to be a danger to their own aircraft?

What country allows non-citizens to enter their branches of armed services?

What country has over 30,000,000 men suffering from impotence?

What country has a southern state where in non-death penalty criminal cases, the jury can convict with only ten of the twelve jurors voting guilty?

What country's citizens purchased almost all of the 22,000,000 Volkswagen Beetles that were produced?

What country sometimes requires prospective pupils to get fifteen shots before they can begin going to public schools?

What country experienced a rash of sixty rapes and murders in 1977 that were thought to have been made by the same "night stalker" who was never caught?

What country has a law in one community that stipulates that released former convicted sex offenders must not turn their lights on on Halloween?

What country used over 50,000,000 tin-plated cans of food daily in the late 1940s?

What country's airlines experienced over 9,000 collisions with birds into jet engines in the year 2002?

What country has to clean up some 60,000 reported toxic spills yearly?

What country has some women opting for foot surgery just so they can fit into fashionable shoes?

What country had an estimated 10,000 GI's go AWOL to Paris when their divisions were chasing the Germans out of France during WWII, and were ordered to divert around the city?

What country expended approximately 25,000 rounds of ammunition during WWII for every enemy killed?

What country passed its military draft law by just one vote in the congress?

What country paid its New York Stock Exchange chairman about $148,000,000 upon his retirement?

What country's Navy was hit with a severe typhoon in the Pacific Ocean in 1944 and had three ships capsized and 790 sailors lost?

What country had 3,000 Catholic parishes without priests in 2003?

What country has twelve people dying daily while they wait for heart transplants?

What country has one state that spends over $900,000,000 on health care for prisoners who are locked up?

What country in the 1950s began a policy of attempting to overthrow governments around the world that they perceived were unfriendly to them?

What country suffered a huge hurricane that destroyed over 110,000 homes?

What country's Red Cross helped in over 70,000 disasters, large and small, around the world in the year 2003?

What country's average youngster is exposed to 10,000 food ads yearly?

What country has convicted over fifty murderers for killing someone when no bodies were ever found?

What country is tied with Mexico for having the highest rate of deaths due to child abuse, among the twenty-seven countries rated?

What country's Catholic archdiocese of a large city agreed to pay $85,000,000 to 552 different people who were victims of sexual abuse?

What country's government provides flood insurance for $645,000,000 worth of beachfront property owned mostly by wealthy people, for well below the market price?

What country estimates the cost of alcoholism to be in excess of $180,000,000 per year . . . more than the cost of all of the other drugs combined?

What country produced about 80,000 Claymore mines during the Viet Nam War that were capable of killing most anything within 100 yards?

What country has a gonorrhea rate that is seventy times the rate in Holland?

What country spent $14,000,000 to prosecute a serial killer who was finally sentenced to death?

What country has held some 660 suspected terrorists from over forty countries in prison in Cuba without any charges or legal representation?

What country had 133,000 incidents of child pornography reported to the authorities over a five-year period?

What country went from spending about $7,000,000,000 on fast foods during the 1970s to over $110,000,000,000 in the 1990s?

What country had more people dying from obesity than from tobacco in 2003?

What country has three times the obesity problem of a country like France?

What country still has over 45,000 troops stationed in Japan, many decades after the end of WWII?

What country sends an estimated 8,000,000 dogs and cats to pounds every year, with approximately 70% being put to death?

What country topples over 4,000,000, on trees every year for lumber?

What country has about 2,300 children reported missing to the FBI daily?

What country estimates that some 923,000,000 people in the world are without a clean source of water, but has no policy to help remedy this?

What country estimates that over 250,000 women will get breast cancer yearly?

What country spends nearly $25,000,000,000 yearly on candy and 60% of it is chocolate?

What country suspended or revoked the licenses of 2,500 educators during 2006–2007 for sexual offenses with children?

What country has about 100 babies who drown in their bathtubs, yearly?

What country has about 600,000 people who are allergic to eggs?

What country has about 1,200,000 people who are allergic to fish?

What country's camps no longer serve peanut butter to their youngsters, even though just about 1% have an allergic reaction to peanuts, but severe reactions kill from 100 to 200 people per year?

What country has just 7% of its people who do not believe in telepathy, ghosts, past lives, or other supernatural phenomena?

What country has one state with over 54,000 registered sex offenders?

What country has a portion of one state where the average rainfall per year is 40′?

What country has estimated that over 80 of its prison population is there due to their addiction to alcohol or drugs?

What country consumes over 1,000,000 boxes of macaroni and cheese every day?

What country performs over 120,000 breast implants yearly?

What country began a superconducting supercollider project that was pushed by politicians, only to shut down the entire project in 1993 after completing fourteen miles of tunneling and spending over $2,000,000,000 on it?

What country has over 47,000,000 people who speak a language other than English at home?

What country consumes 20,000,000,000 hot dogs per year and 127 chickens per second?

What country had an aircraft company that laid off 35,000 employees over a two year period?

What country may have as many as 10,000 tigers in private hands as pets, while there are only an estimated 5,000 left in the wild?

What country was responsible for its citizens forming a mob and murdering the founder of the Mormon religion while he was in jail?

What country, in 2003, had just one state where the governor had a favorable rating from the public of over 50%?

What country has given over $2,500,000,000 to the country of Columbia between 2000 and 2003 for drug enforcement?

What country has one large city that averages over 900 suicides yearly?

What country has a retail giant that serves about 19,000,000 customers every day?

What country has an estimated 100,000 people who enter hospitals without infections, and actually die from infections in those hospitals, yearly?

What country loses seventeen women during infant deliveries per 100,000 births, compared to Canada's rate of six?

What country has an estimated 18,000 people who die yearly due to the lack of any health insurance, according to the Institute of Medicine?

What country loses over 36,000 people annually due to the flu?

What country has about 1,300,000 abortions yearly, and about 2,200 of them the so-called "partial birth" abortions?

What country is planning to move over 140,000,000 pounds of highly radioactive nuclear waste from all over the country, to Yucca mountain, taking from one to six trips daily by train and truck, over twenty-four years?

What country has a survey taken that resulted in just one half of 1% thinking that they would go to hell upon their death?

What country lost over 1,500 people to cholera in their trek west to the gold fields, in the year 1849?

What country lost more soldiers during WWII due to lice and mosquitoes and the diseases they caused, than from bullets?

What country experienced 903,000 victims of child abuse and neglect during the year 2002?

What country has 70% of their kids under the age of two, who spend about two hours each day watching TV?

What country caught a CEO of a top corporation spending $2,100,000 of the company's funds on a birthday party for his wife?

What country had an estimated 370,000 mentally ill people in prisons at a time when there were just 80,000 in mental hospitals?

What country went from an average tuition for a four-year public university of $2,500 in 1993 to over $4,600 ten years later?

What country has estimated that over half of those who should be receiving regular child support payments, will not receive even one payment in any given year?

What country had four out of every ten babies born in 2006 that were out of marriage?

What country between 1882 and 1951 had over 5,000 lynchings and some 75% were of blacks?

What country has 1,800,000 veterans who are uninsured and not eligible for VA care because of their incomes?

What country had forty-two women on death row awaiting execution in 2003?

What country apprehends over 1,000,000 people trying to cross the borders, while over another estimated 1,000,000 are successful yearly?

What country learned that during WWII, only about one in every four infantrymen actually fired at the enemy, while in Viet Nam it was almost 100%?

What country had 101 aircraft carriers towards the end of WWII while the Japanese had just four?

What country has over 95,000,000 people who have invested in mutual funds?

What country initiated an attack on a Cheyenne Indian village in the 1800s at Sand Creek and killed 200 people, mostly women and children?

What country apprehended a serial killer who admitted killing over forty-eight men and women?

What country had 62,000 servicemen who served on PT boats in WWII?

What country has about 63% of its people who want to live past 100?

What country made sensational national heroes out of the Marines who participated in a photo-op and staged second raising of their flag on Iwo Jima, and let the six Marines who actually raised the first flag on Mount Surabachi remain unknown?

What country has about one-half of all hotel guests purchasing porn videos?

What country experienced over 800,000,000 rentals of porn videos during the year 2002 and spends over $10,000,000,000 on "adult entertainment" yearly?

What country has about 150 deaths yearly from vehicle accidents with deer?

What country is performing over 150 stomach by-pass operations yearly on teenagers?

What country has an estimated 300,000 sports-related head injuries yearly?

What country experiences almost 200,000 cases of people contracting Hepatitis A every year?

What country has a database for voluntary hospital reporting where 500 hospitals came forward with 192,0000 admissions of error during 2003, in which the wrong drug was prescribed or the wrong dose?

What country has over 27,000,000 active motorcyclists?

What country had a legislature that levied a $20 per month tax on all "non-Americans" working in the gold mining fields in 1850?

What country had over 600,000 men who perished under President Lincoln's watch?

What country has some 42% of its gasoline stations owned by foreigners?

What country had 58% of black women with jobs in 1940 working as maids, a number that dropped to 1% in 2007?

What country has 25,000 CEOs who are black and over 1,100,000 blacks who earn over $100,000?

What country has over 60,000 babies born every year weighing less than 3.3 pounds?

What country has 1,800,000 people who suffer from diabetes, with that figure expected to double by 2025?

What country has 200,000 people dying from diabetes every year?

What country has a $32,000,000 pizza industry?

What country passed a law in the 1880s that prohibited Mormons from voting, whether or not they practiced polygamy?

What country built a monument to remember the 58,000 servicemen and women who perished in Viet Nam, but has no such memorial for the 3,000,000 Vietnamese who lost their lives in that war?

What country has 16% of its population that have at least one tattoo?

What country had over 1,000 people killed and injured as a result of Firestone tire failures on their vehicles?

What country experiences approximately 130,000 violent criminal acts against school teachers every year by students?

What country, along with Iran and the Congo, has the death penalty for juvenile offenders?

What country has a cigarette lighter company that sells 3,000,000 per day?

What country was recently surpassed by China as the world's biggest recipient of foreign investments?

What country's B-29 pilot during WWII who dropped the first atomic bomb on Hiroshima, killing hundreds of thousands of civilians, was quoted as saying late in life, "I sleep good every night?"

What country's police killed twenty-eight members of the Black Panthers during a two-year period in the 1960s?

What country's police of a large city were sued twelve years after a shootout in an apartment occupied by the Black Panthers involving fourteen police officers, and the city was ordered to pay $1,800,000 in damages to the survivors?

What country has sold over $120,000,000,000 worth of Treasury Bonds to China?

What country injects a genetically engineered growth hormone into about one-third of its dairy herds to increase milk production?

What country has about 6,000 people who die waiting for transplants every year?

What country paid out an average of $1,780,000 to the families of the people killed on 9/11?

What country has refused to support the International Criminal Court because it is afraid that its own citizens may someday be subjected to the punishment meted out by the court?

What country had over 12,000 unsolved murders between 2000 and 2003?

What country had 5,000,000 foreign-born out of 6,000,000 people living in New York City in the year 1919?

What country uprooted over 16,000 Cherokee men, women and children from North Carolina, and marched them some 800 miles to Oklahoma, where only about 3,000 survived?

What country has seen an 84% rise in facelift operations during the last decade?

What country has about 143,000,000 cats and dogs for pets and an additional 43,000,000 other pet animals?

What country has as many as 200,000 adults listed as missing, yearly?

What country had 150,000 of its people visiting Cuba in 2003, one-half of them illegally?

What country had a fast food chain that had to pay out $100,000,000 to victims of their contaminated hamburgers that were not cooked enough?

What country's people spent over $57,000,000 during 2003 for cell phone "original" ring tones?

What country had doctors who perform over 400,000 tonsillectomies every year?

What country has a population where 60% consume alcohol of some kind?

What country has an estimated 28,000,000 suffering from hearing loss?

What country almost annexed the Italian island of Sicily after WWII in 1948?

What country has over 32,000,000 of its people on diets?

What country experienced the death of 686 coal miners in one state during the year 1925?

What country sells potato chips for 200 times the cost of plain potatoes?

What country found a wealthy man not guilty of murder after the trial showed that he had admitted he dismembered the body of a man that he had shot, and put it in the river, beheaded?

What country experienced a tornado in 1925 that killed 695 people and cut a swath of destruction for over 200 miles?

What country's Supreme Court upheld slavery laws during the 1800s, and also upheld the "internment" of the tens of thousands of Japanese at the onset of WWII?

What country had a "watch list" of 1,300,000 potential terrorists in 2003?

What country's population went from almost 50% smokers in 1964 to less than 2% in 2003?

What country's Secretary of State told the United Nations that Iraq had between 100 and 500 tons of chemical weapons prior to the beginning of the war . . . only to find none?

What country bought Alaska from Russia for $7,200,000?

What country had 51,000 men killed, wounded or captured during the three-day battle for Gettysburg?

What country loaned the USSR three icebreaker ships during WWII to enable them to keep their ports open?

What country had a high school raided by eight policemen with weapons drawn and pointed, and leading K-9s, who then handcufffed students and forced them to lie down and spread-eagle, while they searched for drugs, only to find none?

What country has a large city that has spent over $10,000,000 defending a police commander who was accused of torturing some 100 prisoners, and was found guilty in a civil court proceeding?

What country has about 18,000,000 people suffering from sleep apnea?

What country provided Iran with seventy-nine of their top F-14 Navy Tomcat fighter-bomber aircraft in the late 1970s?

What country gave fifty Navy destroyers to Britain to be used in their war against Germany in 1939?

What country had 80,000 licensed gun dealers at one time?

What country reported over 2,000 murders of black men, women and children in one state alone, in the year 1865?

What country has a western state that routinely releases about 1,000 inmates from their jail every week of the year?

What country has almost 25,000,000 small businesses?

What country had about one-third of all children born in 2003 born out of wedlock?

What country spends as much on the military as all 190 other nations, combined?

What country has about 87,000 foot amputations yearly due to diabetes?

What country dropped an estimated 60,000 bombs on one small French town during WWII in an effort to cut German supply lines to submarine bases, destroying 70% of its buildings?

What country had a federal air marshal pull a gun on someone in an airport parking lot for taking his parking place?

What country had a federal air marshall leave his gun in the bathroom on a commercial airliner during a flight?

What country is projected to have over 13,000,000 Alzheimer's patients in the year 2050?

What country's marriage counselors treat an estimated 863,000 married couples per year?

What country had General Custer raid Chief Black Kettle's Indian village where 103 men, women, and children were killed?

What country's scientists have discovered that humans share 97% of their DNA with gorillas?

What country has over 240,000 families with health insurance who still find it necessary to file for bankruptcy yearly, in part due to medical bills?

What country has over 5,000,000 people who have diabetes and don't know it?

What country experienced a rise in health insurance premiums that was six times the rate of inflation?

What country took in 5,000,000 German soldiers who surrendered towards the end of WWII?

What country has over 53,000,000 people who file their income tax returns electronically?

What country has an estimated 4,000,000 new cases of chlamydia, the most common sexually transmitted disease, yearly?

What country has an estimated 27,000,000 people with thyroid disease and about half of them are undiagnosed?

What country has 2,000,000 people walking around with unruptured brain aneurysms?

What country experienced a huge forest fire that consumed 740,000 acres and 3,600 homes?

What country had 283 soldiers who committed suicide after serving in Afghanistan and being discharged within a four-year period after discharge?

What country has used the death penalty for 80% of the time when the victim in a murder is white, and just 14% of the time when the victim is black?

What country back in 1950 had a desert city in the west with an average price of gasoline to be 27¢ a gallon?

What country had a state that passed a law in 2007 that provides for a penalty of one year in prison for a person who gives a ride to an illegal alien?

What country found in 2006 that 49% of accused arsonists were juveniles and 58% of those were fourteen and under?

What country had a financial deficit growing at a rate of $900,000 per minute in early 2004?

What country has 28,000,000 people who suffer from migraine headaches?

What country targeted one of its citizens who was suspected of being an Al Queda terrorist, and launched a missile from an unmanned drone aircraft into Yemen, killing him and five other passengers in the vehicle?

What country has over 2,500,000 grandparents who are raising their grandchildren?

What country's people pay an average of 40% more for their drugs than do people in Canada?

What country's hospitals routinely charge the uninsured patients up to five times the amount they charge their insured patients and those covered by medicare?

What country in 1992 had their top 400 people with the highest incomes averaging about $12,000,000 which in 2002 had grown to $29,000,000?

What country has only 9% of its population that do not have any credit cards?

What country outlawed gambling at horse tracks in the year 1910?

What country had eight major league baseball players in the early 1900s on one team accept a total of $100,000 to throw the world series so gamblers could win money by betting against them?

What country had a serviceman's hotline that received over 30,000 calls from men and women who wanted to get out of the service early in 2003?

What country paid $12,000,000 to the prisoner survivors of the Attica prison riot twenty-six years after it happened?

What country has heart disease as the number-one cause of death for women?

What country had 160 federal marshals wounded during rioting at a southern university, in an effort to get the first black man registered in 1962?

What country suffered the loss of over 500 people during a hurricane that wiped out the Florida Keys highway during its construction?

What country launched a bombing attack from England to Germany during WWII with 870 planes dropping incendiary bombs over a period of 4 days and killing an estimated 100,000 civilians?

What country's general decided to allow the Russians to take Berlin at the end of WWII after learning that it might cost 100,000 lives to take the city?

What country launched 1000 heavy bombers in an attack on Berlin on Hitler's birthday, dropping thousands of tons of bombs on the crumbling city just three weeks before the end of the war?

What country conducted the war crimes trial at Nuremberg after WWII, and after 200 days of trial, the verdict was to hang twelve and acquit three highly ranked Germans?

What country allows the results of polygraph tests to be shown in court provided that both parties agreed prior to the administering of the test?

What country discovered 285 tons of gold bars and coins in an underground salt mine in the Soviet sector of Germany during the final days of WWII and had it all transferred to their sector?

What country ordered 200 of the finest art masterpieces found in Germany during WWII to be shipped back to their country, but returned them three years later?

What country decided to allow the Germans to try their own war criminals after WWI, only to find that it turned into a big fiasco?

What country tried and convicted two army officers of looting millions of dollars of the Hess crown jewels during and after WWII only to have them say at their trial that they were just doing what everyone else was doing?

What country has 800,000 men taking prescription testosterone supplements?

What country has a fleet of 18 nuclear submarines that can carry the equivalent of 23,000 atomic bombs of the type that leveled Hiroshima?

What country has spent over $800,000,000 on submarines since 1950?

What country inserted escape devices into Red Cross packages that were destined for POWs held by the Germans during WWII?

What country has over 3,000,000 people on court-ordered probation at any one time?

What country went from having 7% illegal immigrants working in agriculture in 1989 to 55% in 2003?

What country suffered the loss of over 700 sailors on board an aircraft carrier during WWII after two hits by Japanese kamikaze aircraft?

What country has estimated that somewhere around 16,000,000 people lost their lives during WWII?

What country discovered some fifty V-2 rockets in Germany during WWII and surreptitiously moved them from the Russian sector to theirs?

What country puts approximately 5,000,000 dogs to death, yearly?

What country had a sitting president who was forty-nine years old and married a twenty-one-year-old woman?

What country had a president who took 399 train rides during his time in office?

What country has 4,000,000 people under the age of sixty-five that require long-term care, either in skilled nursing facilities or at home?

What country went from an average daily per person calorie intake count of 3200 in 1975, to 3900 in the year 2000?

What country began drinking more soda than milk in the year 1976, and in the year 2003 the figure is twice as much soda?

What country had over 1,000,000 new homes purchased in 2003 at an average price of $250,000?

What country has about 2,000 babies who die from sudden infant death syndrome yearly, and another 900 suffocate in soft bedding?

What country and their allies had fifty airmen executed by the German Gestapo for their attempted escape from a prison camp in WWII?

What country had the average height of its citizens increase by five inches over the past 100 years?

What country had a B-29 on a secret mission in 1948 crash into Lake Mead while flying low over it, because the pilot was reading the instruments based upon sea level, not the higher level of the lake?

What country is experiencing over 480,000,000 hits per year on on-line dating sites?

What country suffers about 1,000 deaths and 20,000 injuries due to police chases, yearly?

What country has over 1,000,000 children being raised in gay families?

What country has a mining industry that has cut its labor force 80% over the past few decades, and yet is producing more metals than ever before?

What country has 587,000 abandoned mine sites that must be cleaned up at taxpayers expense?

What country has over 1,000,000 people quitting their jobs every week?

What country torpedoed and sank a Japanese ship during WWII only to find out later that the ship carried thousands of POWs?

What country has hospital-acquired infections that add almost $5,000,000,000 to the nation's yearly health care cost?

What country has more people dying from hospital-acquired infections than from vehicle accidents and homicides combined?

What country captured over 10,000 enemies in Afghanistan, sent 650 of them to Guantanamo, Cuba, and months later released eighty-seven?

What country had many contributors to the presidential campaign of 2000 of over $100,000, and twenty-one of them became ambassadors after the election?

What country came very close to war with the USSR in the early 1960s when opposing tanks faced each other at checkpoint Charlie in Berlin?

What country's people experience over 700,000 strokes per year, that result in over 165,000 deaths?

What country has projected that 1,000,000 species will be extinct in the year 2050 if global warming trends continue?

What country had 346 complaints of broadcast indecency in 2001 and 250,000 complaints in 2003?

What country has a college football coach who makes $2,500,000 per year while the average salary of many college professors is $85,000?

What country has 50,000 of its citizens living in the area of Guadalajara, Mexico?

What country lost a U-2 spy plane to missiles over both Cuba and the USSR during the late 1950s?

What country has estimated that some 40,000,000 children will be orphaned by AIDS worldwide, by the year 2010?

What country had fifty-six law enforcement officers killed on duty in 2002?

What country had a former president who traveled to Africa on a hunting expedition and took along twenty-four reporters and photographers?

What country has about 40,000 of its citizens who were born male, have had the necessary surgery to make them females?

What country loses about 1,000,000,000 birds every year due to flying into glass?

What country has hunters killing about 121,000,000 birds every year?

What country outsourced over 140,000 jobs to India in 2003 and has estimated that by the year 2015 there will be over 3,000,000 jobs outsourced to other lands?

What country took over 100 years to ratify the last amendment to its constitution?

What country went from performing 2,000,000 cosmetic procedures in 1997, to 8,300,000 in 2003?

What country has one-half of their new teachers leaving their jobs within the first five years?

What country is buying unmanned aircraft for the military at $40,000,000 per plane?

What country has over 10,000,000 motorists who display a small E-Z Pass tag on their windshield that allows them to coast through toll booths, by paying electronically?

What country suffered the execution of ninety-eight civilian POWs on Wake Island after they were tied up and blindfolded by the Japanese in 1943?

What country made a wartime propaganda movie showing that all their soldiers died fighting bravely to the end at Wake Island, when in fact, some 1600 surrendered to the Japanese?

What country had a large city's city council pass an ordinance against anyone wearing a so-called "zoot suit" in 1943, that carried a sentence of thirty days in jail?

What country suffered five civilian casualties from a balloon bomb that landed in Oregon, one of 9,000 such bombs released by Japan in WWII?

What country kept secret until after WWII that a balloon bomb launched from Japan had exploded in Detroit?

What country's Catholic Church has spent some $572,000,000 on lawyers' fees, settlements, and therapy for abuse victims, and treatment for priests?

What country has its average citizen on video 36 times a day?

What country lost over 1,000 people in the torpedo sinking of the Lusitania by a German U-boat prior to the start of WWI?

What country spends over $1,000,000,000 per day on its military?

What country uses an estimated average of 100 million gallons of fuel per year for each domestic commercial airliner flying?

What country has up to 1,000,000 words in their language, while a country like France has just 125,000?

What country has some 100,000,000 bats that migrate up from Mexico every spring, and flying at 10,000 feet can create a danger to aircraft?

What country had LSD as a legal drug during the 1960s?

What country had a national survey that categorized 64% of its women as "pear-shaped?"

What country has almost 19,000,000 new cases of sexually transmitted diseases each year?

What country has over 23,000,000 young people who are eligible to vote but are not registered?

What country had one state that made over 15,000 arrests of speeders who were going over 100 miles per hour in 2003?

What country began a program in 2002 that for ten years will give farmers $200,000,000 in direct government handouts, and another $200,000,000 in artificial price supports?

What country had about 749,000,000 acres of forest land in 2003 compared to about 734,000,000 acres in the 1920s?

What country allowed its people for the first 140 years to use any chemical they wanted on themselves and did not make opium illegal until 1914?

What country has an estimated 10,000 people stung by scorpions yearly?

What country stopped producing all convertible automobiles during the years 1976 and 1982?

What country arrested over 10,000 medical doctors during the first five years of the passage of the Harrison Act in 1914 that made some drugs illegal?

What country arrests more than 500,000 youngsters yearly for smoking pot?

What country consumes 5,000,000,000 tranquilizers, 5,000,000,000 barbiturates and 3,000,000,000 amphetamines per year?

What country consumes over 16,000 tons of aspirins every year?

What country gains a person every twelve seconds counting births and immigration, and taking into consideration deaths?

What country has over 90,000,000 owners of leaf-blowers?

What country patented over 500 different kinds of barbed wire, mostly in the late 1800s?

What country adds $300,000,000 yearly to its trucking industry costs for every penny increase in the cost of fuel?

What country stood by in 1994 while some 800,000 men, women and children were butchered in 100 days of Rwanda's civil war?

What country had most of its senior citizens in the 1950s with false or no teeth?

What country has about 60% women going to college and 40% men?

What country has the technology to stretch just one ounce of gold wire for 50 miles?

What country had one of its citizens invent, design and manufacture the famous Duesenburg automobile?

What country experiences over 1,000 tornadoes that touch down yearly?

What country has a list of some 55,000 names of individuals living in other countries who are not allowed into the country because they are suspected terrorists?

What country had over 140,000,000 people clicking on to on-line dating in 2003?

What country has an estimated 75% of all people who get their driver's license suspended, ignore it and continue to drive?

What country has 25 states with laws similar to "three strikes and you're out"?

What country has seen since the 1970s, the amount of an average family budget earmarked for their mortgage, increase by 69%, while the average father's income has increased just less than 1%?

What country had an estimated 400,000 deaths during the year 2000 that were attributed to rich diets and sedentary lifestyles?

What country imposed mandatory drug tests upon its soldiers who were ready to leave Viet Nam, and if they failed it, they could not return home?

What country added the phrase "Under God" to its Pledge of Allegiance in 1954?

What country is eating 42% more imported food now, than twenty years ago?

What country has only about 8,000 bodies donated to science yearly?

What country had twelve bull riders killed in just one year?

What country fired 1,200 airport screeners after background checks revealed they had lied on their applications, or had a criminal history?

What country had a state prison system where the cost of incarcerating each prisoner went from $150 per year, to over $30,000 over a period of years?

What country had 12,000 teens who pledged to remain virgins until marriage, only to have a study reveal that 88% went ahead and had premarital sex?

What country has over 54,000,000 of its people on diets?

What country only audits six or seven income tax returns out of every 1,000 personal returns?

What country had one city that issued over 7,000 medical marijauna ID cards, permitting them to obtain the drug?

What country has one in every four births a C-section?

What country had 60% of all companies that paid no income tax at all, from the years 1996 to 2000?

What country gave Pakistan $150,000,000 per month in aid in 2007?

What country had a president who declared in a public speech that three countries were the "Axis of Evil"?

What country turned the tiny island of Iwo Jima back to Japan in 1993?

What country has about 1,200 actors who are tested for VD and AIDS each month of the year, in the porn movie industry?

What country uses over 26,000,000,000 rolls of toilet tissue yearly?

What country has one in every 250 children born, diagnosed with autism?

What country in its early years executed nineteen women for consorting with the devil?

What country lost 749 servicemen during a dress rehearsal for the Normandy invasion when the Germans spotted "Exercise Tiger," and for morale purposes it was kept quiet by the government for two decades?

What country had a president who declared in a public speech that the other super power was an "Evil Empire?"

What country in 1835 drove the Mexicans out of the Alamo, and out of Texas?

What country in 1836 witnessed 4,000 Mexican soldiers under their general Santa Anna march into San Antonio and threaten to drive all the way to Washington?

What country has over 1,000,000 children who are not fully immunized?

What country had a president, in a public speech, declare to his terrorist enemies, "Bring it on"?

What country has about 100,000,000 of its people visiting emergency wards of hospitals, yearly?

What country has estimated that there are about 106,000 power tool accidents that require medical attention, yearly?

What country, during the 1800s, had their pharmacies selling alcoholic beverages?

What country awarded 464 Congressional Medals of Honor during WWII?

What country has over 750,000 people on parole from prison at all times?

What country has over 1,000,000 illegal immigrants living in just one city?

What country lynched an estimated 5,000 Negroes during the years 1880 through 1930, without any trials?

What country has a drug industry that employs 750 political lobbyists?

What country passed a prescription drug bill that was touted to cost about $395,000,000,000 over the first ten years, only to find out after it passed in Congress, that the estimate should have been $534,000,000,000?

What country experienced 24,703 murders during the year 2003?

What country has heart disease as the number-one killer of women?

What country has 6,400,000 of its people working for foreign-owned companies?

What country had 24% of its servicemen who were killed during "Desert Storm" action in Kuwait, killed by friendly fire?

What country has about 720 infant deaths per year that could all be prevented if all babies were breast-fed from birth?

What country has a city that arrests over 600 people per year for cheating at gambling games?

What country imprisoned over 43,000 Iraqis without charges during the first year of the Iraq war, and subsequently released 27,000 of them?

What country has estimated that 30% of all marriages between immigrants and citizens are fraudulent?

What country's people buy more bottle water than coffee, milk or beer?

What country had about 7,000,000 people with cell phones in 2003 and forecast that another 15,000,000 would be added by 2004?

What country had over 14,000,000 documents classified as "SECRET" in 2003?

What country had a CEO of a major commercial airline company who handed out bonuses to his top executives at the same time that he eliminated 14,000 jobs and was negotiating for $1,800,000,000 in salary cuts to his work force?

What country experiences 330,000 injuries per year and some 2,600 traffic deaths resulting from cell phone usage while driving?

What country lost 724 men on one aircraft carrier due to a WWII kamikaze attack by Japanese planes?

What country's navy lost 5,000 men and another 5,000 wounded during the sea battles for the island of Iwo Jima during WWII?

What country is financing a TV station by the tune of $60,000,000 for just one year, to broadcast into Iraq and other Arab countries?

What country has about 4,000,000 people who turn 18 every year?

What country lost 1,177 servicemen when a ship sank in nine minutes during the attack on Pearl Harbor by the Japanese?

What country fired at and sank a midget Japanese submarine near Pearl Harbor about an hour prior to the air attack, but the Navy brass was skeptical of the report and did not sound an alarm of the impending attack?

What country prosecuted an environmental organization for boarding a ship that was carrying endangered trees that were illegally felled?

What country had 127,677 prison inmates who were serving life sentences at a cumulative cost of $2,500,000,000 to taxpayers in 2004?

What country has a state that allows first cousins to marry if they are over 65 years of age?

What country had a president of a company who received $109,300,000 in severance pay after being fired in 1996?

What country has about 1,000,000 people who develop skin cancer yearly?

What country lost 689 people to multiple tornadoes in one day in 1925?

What country has a city that gets over 30,000,000 visitors yearly and who lose over $7,000,000,000 by gambling?

What country had an estimated 4,500,000 people suffering from Alzheimer's disease in 2004?

What country had 51,000,000 of its registered voters stay home during the election of 2000?

What country spends $3,000,000,000 yearly on recruiting for the military?

What country suffered 167 miners killed in a mine fire caused by a carbide lamp in 1917?

What country had Martha Stewart in prison at the same time O.J. Simpson was on a golf course?

What country's Food and Drug Administration received over 17,000 complaints of adverse health reactions to ephedra, including strokes, seizures, and deaths before imposing a ban?

What country has many of its people believing that it gives about 15% of its GNP to foreign aid, while it actually contributes about 1/10th of 1%?

What country experienced a steamboat disaster in 1904 that claimed the life of 1,021 people including 800 children?

What country has over 60,000,000 Catholics?

What country loses 900 young children yearly to drowning?

What country has 535 men and women serving in Congress, but only one who has a son serving in the Iraq war?

What country has 1,300,000 cases of skin cancer every year?

What country has an estimated 3,000,000 people who admit to ''swinging''?

What country annually conducts tests for cancer of the cervix on about 10,000,000 women who have previously had their cervix removed?

What country had 80% of their youngsters playing sports every day in 1969 and only 20% doing the same in 2004?

What country paid out over 5,800 claims to the tune of over $4,000,000 to Iraqi civilians for various misdeeds by its military during the first year of occupation?

175

What country conducted a survey that concluded that only one in four infantrymen actually fired at the enemy during WWII?

What country overturned over 140 convictions of serious crimes due to DNA findings, including thirteen who had been sentenced to die, as of 2004?

What country has nearly 95% of all felony crimes plea bargained down?

What country had 9,300 emergency room visits for injuries suffered from Fourth of July fireworks in the year 2003?

What country has over 95% of all foreign trade passing through its ports?

What country had its pharmaceutical companies agree to pay $2,000,000,000 to settle allegations of illegal sales and marketing practices since 2001?

What country increased its total spending on pharmaceutical promotions by 93% between 1997 and 2002?

What country has an army of pharmaceutical lobbyists encamped in its capitol to make sure no harmful legislation to the industry is ever passed?

What country has an average of 161 people who lose their lives in traffic accidents every July 4th?

What country conducted an experiment with syphilis upon blacks in Tuskegee and intentionally withheld treatment that was available, requiring a presidential apology decades later?

What country has found that men over twenty-one years of age are three times more likely to father children with high school girls, than younger boys?

What country considered homosexuality a ''psychiatric disorder'' until late in the 20th century?

What country has over 35,000 Elvis impersonators?

What country has just one state in the entire nation that requires physical education in school in grades K through 12?

What country auctioned off over 450,000 vehicles on eBay during 2003?

What country had a monopoly on nonflammable helium and would not supply it to Germany for their airship the Hindenberg, in the late 1930s?

What country discovered over 1,000 painting masterpieces and 100 tons of gold bullion in an underground salt mine in Germany during the closing days of WWII?

What country consumes about 150,000,000 hot dogs every Fourth of July?

What country passed a 2004 corporate tax bill in the House of Representatives that would give tobacco farmers $9,600,000,000 over a five-year period?

What country killed 3,500,000 buffalo during a ten-year period?

What country arrests about 3,000 illegal aliens every day of the year?

What country purchased 1,000 Luger pistols from Germany in the early 1900s?

What country has over 4,000,000 of its people who have been infected with the Hepatitis C virus with some 30,000 more becoming infected yearly?

What country recalled 150,000,000 bracelets, rings and necklaces for having dangerous levels of lead, in 2003?

What country experienced an earthquake measured at 9.2 on the Richter scale that created a 210' high tsunami that lifted a 7,000 ton ship to the top of buildings, leaving 131 dead and over 5,000 homeless?

What country has found out that up to 40% of all appendectomies turn out to be unnecessary?

What country has estimated that 150 tons of cocaine comes across its borders and into the country every year?

What country in the 1880s thought that cocaine was a good drug for baseball players to be taking?

What country outlawed the use of cocaine after it became believed that violence upon whites was being caused by Negroes taking the drug?

What country has over 700,000,000,000 of its dollars in circulation?

What country has one large county that has from 50,000 to 80,000 homeless people on any given day?

What country helped to arrange the overthrow of democratically elected President Mosadegh of Iran, and then supported the autocratic Shah of Iran for many years?

What country has a Glacier National Park that has gone from 150 glaciers to just twenty over the past decades?

What country had one in every 67 households filing for bankruptcy in 2003?

What country had tea as the national beverage until their Civil War?

What country and its allies lost 6,500 ships to German U-boats in WWII?

What country voted for liquor prohibition partly due to the anti-German hysteria and the dominance of German beermakers?

What country rescinded the prohibition of liquor partly as an effort to bring the nation back from a recession?

What country has deer related accidents that cost over $1,000,000,000?

What country had auto accidents during the year 2000 that cost over $230,000,000,000?

What country went from six weeks for an average hospital staff for a heart attack in the 1950s, to six days some 50 years later?

What country has over 1,000,000 people under the age of 18 taking anti-depressants?

What country had over 84,000 kids who suffered trampoline injuries during 2001?

What country has about 50,000,000 people who qualify as "disabled" under the "Americans with Disabilities Act"?

What country lost over 1,000 steamboats due to river snags on the Missouri river during the 1930s?

What country has over 275 elected officials who are openly gay?

What country has over 8,000,000 overuse injuries such as swimmer's shoulder and gymnast's knee, mostly due to youngsters' intense training?

What country during WWII developed a project where a large number of Mexican bats were outfitted with incendiary bombs attached to their bellies?

What country suffered 1,201 train accidents during the year 1875?

What country has over 50,000,000 so-called "birders"?

What country's airport security prevented Ted Kennedy from getting on a flight because his name resembled the alias of a suspected terrorist?

What country, a few months prior to 9/11, gave the Afghan Taliban government $43,000,000 for cutting back on opium production?

What country spent almost $11,000,000,000 on credit card fees in 2004?

What country continued to use an aircraft after it had experienced 148 non-combat major accidents, with forty pilots killed?

What country performs over 500,000 heart bypass operations yearly?

What country had 27% millionaires attending the 2004 Republican convention?

What country's people spend about $12,400,000,000 on drugs to treat depression yearly?

What country had 19 children die due to being left in the car during hot weather in 2003?

What country had 91 children die in 2003 due to auto back-overs?

What country's airport security collected some 13,000,000 items in 2006 and turned them over to state surplus property agencies where they end up being sold online or at retail stores?

What country had seven children die in 2003 due to being strangled by power windows on vehicles?

What country had over 32,000,000 people who have opted for full-body scans at 100 times the radiation of a normal mammogram?

What country provided a heart transplant operation for a prisoner who was convicted of armed robbery, at a cost of $900,000, while about 4,000 people were still on the waiting list?

What country has about 14,000,000 adult children living at home with parents with little or no intention of moving out?

What country's military, in its infancy, fled from a British invasion force of 5,000 and left the capital building and White House unprotected, to be burned to the ground?

What country invaded Canada and attacked the city of York during the War of 1812?

What country surrendered their Detroit fortress of 2,000 men to the British during the War of 1812 without firing a shot?

What country now has about 70% double-income families?

What country experienced a hurricane in the year 1900 and 8,000 people died, including ninety children in an orphanage along with ten nuns?

What country spends $10,000,000 per week helping Colombia with a drug problem?

What country has estimated that 440,000 of its people die yearly from smoking?

What country has a company that produces over 100,000 slot machines every year?

What country estimates that casinos' slot machine profits amount to about $20,000,000,000 per year?

What country has one out of every four large companies who insure some of their employees and make themselves the beneficiaries, unbeknownst to the employees?

What country has police pursuits that result in over 300 deaths per year?

What country has some of its hospitals who mark up their supplies and services up to 673% to their patients who do not have any insurance?

What country has an estimated 400,000 rebuilt auto wrecks being sold at salvage auctions and put back on the road, yearly?

What country has over 4,600 obsolete military aircraft being stored in the desert worth some untold billions of dollars?

What country has an estimated one in five children who use a computer on chat lines who have been sexually solicited on line?

What country has an estimated 50,000 sexual predators on line using computers?

What country has had an 8,000 pound nuclear bomb missing since it was jettisoned after an in-air craft collision off the coast of Georgia in 1958?

What country has a city that suffered 727 unsolved murders during 1998?

What country has had more than thirteen women and children die from having their hair sucked into the drains of their hot tubs?

What country experiences about 360,000 violent crimes with guns yearly?

What country had 146,000,000 cell phones in operation at the same time that China had 175,000,000?

What country passed a law during WWII that encouraged farm laborers in Mexico to come and harvest its crops, to replace those who were drafted?

What country had almost 15,000,000 men in uniform at the end of WWII?

What country, since 1938, has applied a compound of "rubbing mud" that is taken from a secret location to all of the new baseballs used in major league games, amounting to 1,000,000 balls yearly?

What country has more people declaring bankruptcy yearly than those who graduate from college?

What country had a city pay a street cop over $147,000 in one year due to overtime?

What country has a prison that covers an area of 18,000 acres?

What country finds an average of two one-hundredths of an ounce of gold for every ton of ore they process?

What country had 100,000,000 square miles of public land in 1872?

What country has about 250,000 abandoned mining sites?

What country has 13,500,000 custodial parents of whom just 15% are male?

What country has more women and girls attempting suicide than men and boys, but they are successful much less often?

What country has a huge dump truck that has tires that weigh 26,000 pounds, each?

What country has discharged over 10,000 service men and women who have violated the ''don't ask, don't tell'' policy?

What country spent $14,000,000 prosecuting a multiple murder?

What country has about 117,000 children in its foster care system who are available for adoption yearly?

What country had seventy-four juveniles on death row in 2004?

What country had over 300,000 violent attacks upon correction officers in prisons during a six-year period?

What country had over 20,000 names on its ''no fly'' list in 2004 and is adding over 300 names per day?

What country experiences about 4,700,000 dog bites in a typical year?

What country had, at one time in its Civil War, more soldiers suffering from venereal diseases than wounded by the enemy?

What country had one gambling casino that had 1,500 working cameras at any one time?

What country had a court case where 95,000 black farmers were awarded $50,000 each for discrimination, in 1998?

What country has had over 20,000 women use the RU486 so-called abortion pill?

What country's president assigned escort war ships to accompany British ships crossing the Atlantic ocean, prior to its entry into WWII?

What country provided a severance package amounting to $140,000,000 to a Disney executive who was leaving the company?

What country lost 129 sailors in 1963 who were aboard a nuclear sub when it sank?

What country has spent over $800,000,000,000 on submarines since about 1950?

What country banned liquor in the early 1920s but allowed marijuana to remain legal until 1924?

What country's first president produced 11,000 gallons of whiskey in his later years?

What country spent $80,000,000 on TV ads during just the last few days of the 2004 presidential campaign?

What country has men having about 18% of all cosmetic surgeries?

What country did not declare war after a German submarine sank one of its destroyers, killing all aboard, in 1941?

What country spends over $7,500,000,000 prosecuting and imprisoning about 724,000 yearly for possession of marijuana?

What country has a law where any high school student caught with marijuana cannot get federal aid for college, but has no such provision for those who commit violent crimes?

What country has a professional baseball player who signed a contract for $252,000,000?

What country lost 36,000 of its people to the flu in 2003?

What country fired over 600 tons of shells containing depleted uranium from its aircraft and tanks in the Iraq war?

What country lost 127 men in just one day who were imprisoned in 1864 at Andersonville?

What country experienced fourteen box cars full of bombs, blowing up one after another in 1973?

What country sent eight Marines in 1805 to hire a mercenary army in an attempt to overthrow the leader of Tripoli but ended up paying $60,000 for the release of 300 prisoners and abandoned the attempt?

What country has a national park that sits on a volcano that covers an expanse of forty miles by thirty-five miles?

What country had over 100,000 black women reported missing in 1999?

What country had 162 women raped in one city, in just one month?

What country has a city with 8,000,000 people and over 5,000,000 pets?

What country has suicide as the second leading cause of death among its college students?

What country sells about 40,000,000 cases of vodka every year?

What country has about 4,000,000 members of the NRA?

What country used thousands of Sherman tanks during WWII, that after the war, many experts declared were almost criminal to put into service?

What country put eighteen Sherman tanks into a battle with the Germans during WWII, and had seventeen of them blow up?

What country had a president named Eisenhower lobby his Supreme Court Chief Justice to uphold the doctrine of "separate but equal'' to keep black children out of schools attended by whites?

What country had about 167,000 foreign babies adopted by its people during the period 1989 to 2002?

What country tried, convicted and sent to prison thirty-nine people for child sex abuse after hearing convincing testimony from the children, only to have twenty-two eventually released after children recanted their testimony?

What country used plastic cards more often that cash to buy goods and services in 2003?

What country experienced a bank holdup by an eighty-six year-old man?

What country had 120 babies drown while they were using baby bath seats that were held to the side of bathtubs with suction cups, between 1983 and 2004?

What country had a submarine that had to return to port after a chunk was bitten out of its neoprene bow by a shark?

What country had its first president who had false teeth, not made from wood, but from hippo's teeth?

What country has about 32,000,000 people with false teeth?

What country has about seventeen deaths from dog bites yearly, out of about 4,700,000 bites?

What country has a population that chews over 50,000,000 sticks of gum per day?

What country has over 14,000,000 people battling alcoholism?

What country still had a law on its books in a major city in 2003 that authorized the arrest of any Indian found within its city limits?

What country has estimated that there are over 40,000,000 worldwide who are living with HIV in 2004?

What country had one state with eight women on death row in 2004?

What country passed a $7,000,000,000 lend-lease agreement with Britain nine months before December, 1941, which was six times their entire military budget just three years before?

What country had over 8,200,000 households with a net worth of over $1,000,000 in 2004?

What country had drug companies spending $16,400,000,000 on free samples of their drugs in 2003?

What country imports about 80% of all seafood sold?

What country has about half of its population that does not have a single dollar put away for retirement?

What country has about 1,000,000 retirees being paid pensions by the government guarantee agency due to company bankruptcies?

What country has an estimated 8,000,000 adults with attention deficit disorder?

What country has 88% of teens who have premarital sex after taking the virginity pledge?

What country passed a law in 1873 making all forms of preventing births, illegal?

What country produces over 700,000,000 condoms every year?

What country's Pentagon spent $50,000,000 for Viagra for the troops and for their veterans?

What country loses about 9,000 people yearly to food poisoning?

What country, according to its Pentagon, had 5,500 GIs desert during the first two years of the Iraq war?

What country had over 55,000 estimated deserters during the course of the Viet Nam war?

What country has about 1,200 people dying from the use of tobacco products every day?

What country had a town with a church for sale, but when some Muslims bid on it, the city council voted to give them $100,000 to withdraw their bid?

What country has about 6,000,000 Jews and an equal number of Muslims?

What country wanted to hang 307 Dakota Indians for an uprising in 1862, but only obtained permission from the President to hang thirty-eight?

What country has 2,000,000 people who are allergic to bee venom?

What country has over 192,000,000 privately owned firearms?

What country has 4,300,000 women motorcycle drivers?

What country had a typical fast food hamburger weigh one ounce in 1957, and six ounces in 1997?

What country has just one state with 631 men on death row in prison?

What country has firefighters engaged in fighting fires just 13% of the time?

What country has had over 2,000,000 women with breast augmentation surgery?

What country has an average consumption of carbonated soft drinks that amounts to the equivalent of 574 cans per person, per year?

What country has about 73,000,000 pet cats?

What country has about 1,500,000 pet snakes kept in homes?

What country had the average age of the new car buyer at forty-seven in 2004?

What country had drivers over seventy years of age involved in accidents during the year 2003, with 4,800 deaths and 145,000 injuries?

What country has over 500,000 hysterectomies performed on women per year?

What country can have a person go to the hospital with a nosebleed and come out with bills amounting to $44,000?

What country has 48,000,000 people receiving Social Security benefits?

What country has over 750,000 ham radio enthusiasts?

What country has two states where it is a criminal offense to give someone a tattoo?

What country experienced over 476,000 deaths due to cancer in 2002?

What country experienced over 3,000 unsolved murders over a fourteen-year period, in just one county?

What country has some 750,000 ex-convicts out on parole at any one time?

What country has high medical costs contributing to over half of all bankruptcies?

What country has some 35,000,000 people who just pay the required minimum payment on their credit card balances every month?

What country has about 144,000,000 of its people with credit cards?

What country has 55,000,000 people who pay off their entire credit card balance every month?

What country has some credit card companies that charge up to 29% in interest, even when the prime rate is as low as 2% or 3%?

What country had an average yearly family income of $4,300 in 1953?

What country's space shuttle burns up 20,000 pounds of fuel for every second of its ascent into space?

What country began a fast food operation in 1948 that now has 30,000 franchise outlets in 100 different countries?

What country had a millionaire pass away and leave $50,000,000 to the poor kids of Panama, only to have one of Panama's most prominent and politically connected families attempt to void the gift through their courts?

What country has a giant retail store that is routinely criticized for its low paid employees, but had an average wage in 2007 of $10.74, which is far above the legal minimum wage?

What country has a giant retailer that increased its $4 generic drug price policy to include 361 drugs in 2007?

What country has a major manufacturer of aircraft that is working on a commercial airliner that was available in 2008, and has fifty customers who have ordered $120,000,000,000 worth of the plane, a year ahead of its availability?

What country had an auto manufacturer who had a $39,000,000,000 loss in just the period between July to September 2007?

What country had circumcision fall from 85% of all newborn boys in 1965 to just 57% in 2005, and is no longer routinely covered by Medicaid?

What country had a popular professional basketball star produce a quality sneaker for about $15 to compete with others that cost up to $175?

What country has the average cost of a meal in a restaurant in one of its largest cities, going for $143?

What country had a CEO of a huge brokerage company retire with a package of over $161,000,000 after his firm took a loss of almost $8,000,000,000 of its assets due to bad bets on mortgage-related securities?

What country has discovered that home appliances left on standby waste 5% of the country's electricity at a cost of $4,000,000,000 per year?

What country had a phone company that faced a proposed fine of over $17,000,000 in one state for poor service during the first five months of 2006?

What country had its average farm family getting 82% of its income from non-farm sources, in 2007?

What country finds its median farmer enjoying five times the net worth of the median non-farmer household, in 2007?

What country was finalizing a $286,000,000,000 farm bill in its congress in 2007?

What country's government accounting office discovered that $1,100,000,000 in farm subsidies have been paid to dead people?

What country's farm lobby spent $135,000,000 on lobbying and "donations" during 2006?

What country paid its largest recipient of farm subsidies $531,000,000 since 1995?

What country has invented a laser-guided launcher mounted on the front grille of cop cars that tags a fleeing vehicle with a GPS tracking device, so that they can hang back as the real time location of the vehicle is sent to police headquarters?

What country had three of every ten military recruits requiring waivers to get into the service in 2007 mostly due to drug and other criminal records?

What country's public was asked in 2007 if they favored an air strike into Iran and some 30% were in favor of it, with some 23% favoring an invasion by ground troops?

What country had veterans comprising over 25% of all homeless people in 2007?

What country has about 80% of its people living paycheck to paycheck?

What country's "no fly" list has ballooned to 750,000 names, and 20,000 more are added every month?

What country has a women's prison with over 1,600 inmates?

What country has a women's prison where an inmate who has a baby while incarcerated can keep the baby there in prison for up to one year?

What country had a woman in a large women's prison, who had nine little children at home while she was serving time?

What country has a state that holds primary residential election caucuses before any other state and has a record of picking the winners about 60% of the time, and yet only one of twenty-nine eligible voters ever turn out to vote?

What country has a state with an early primary presidential election caucus whose results are widely thought to be very influential throughout the nation, and yet the average voter is in his or her fifties?

What country had a drug company that provided a very popular drug to over 20,000,000 people, but learned that it could cause heart attacks and strokes and was sued by 50,000 people . . . and settled for $4,850,000,000?

What country, in 2007, detained 17,000 new Iraqi insurgents, and is still holding over 25,800 without trials?

What country had a first base coach of a professional baseball team, hit by a line drive in the neck and killed?

What country's servicemen in Iraq are experiencing some 84% with receiving hostile fire and returning fire . . . never before seen in any war?

What country has almost half of all inmates who are released on parole from prisons returned within the first twelve months?

What country initiated a system whereby points were assessed for some 25,000 foods based upon healthiness, the good receiving one star, better, getting two, and best getting three stars, and after checking the stars earned at supermarkets found that 73% earned no stars at all?

What country is offering $5,000 to farmers to install wind-energy turbines, as opposed to making maybe $300 for corn or soybeans?

What country has a mega-internet company that offers its employees seventeen no-cost dining areas, each focused on a specific cuisine, along with swimming pools, health clinics, volley ball courts and massage rooms?

What country, back in 1904, recommended 45 minutes of penmanship curriculum per day to its students, and in 2007 has decreased to 10?

What country had one of its citizens develop a flashlight for the 1,600,000,000 people in the world without electric lights, that runs on solar power?

What country has preschools that cost parents $23,000 per year for their three-year-olds?

What country had 69% of its four-year-olds attending preschools in 2005?

What country has a restaurant that provides an eight-ounce Japanese Wagyu ribeye steak to its customers for $160?

What country has nearly 15% of its active duty military personnel, females?

What country has 60% of its churchgoers female?

What country's average household uses about 100,000 gallons of water every year?

What country has 300,000 people who break a hip yearly?

What country has some 750,000 people who are no longer able to work and are waiting for up to three years for hearings to receive Social Security disability payments?

What country has its largest candy maker closing some plants, laying off 1,500 people, and moving some operations to Mexico?

What country has many of its scientists now believing that 68,000,000 years ago, a huge asteroid hit the earth and about 300,000 years later volcano eruptions put the finishing touches to the mass extinction of dinosaurs?

What country attributes most calamities and catastrophes to "Mother Nature"?

What country had a $100 price for a barrel of oil in 1980, adjusted for yearly inflation?

What country's life expectancy in 2007 was at its highest ever, at 78, and yet still trails forty-three other nations, including Jordan, Bosnia, and Herzegovina?

What country's veterans comprise just 11% of the population, but 26% of the nation's homeless?

What country's military approved the sale of "Playboy" and "Penthouse" magazines on their bases, after a decade-long ban?

What country has about 400,000 people who are full time RVers?

What country had a 22% increase in the sales of RVs priced at over $550,000 in 2006?

What country's RV resorts are beginning to charge overnight fees of about $50 per night for hookups?

What country has an estimated 3,000,000 adults who are considered "gender variant"?

What country's children who are "gender variant" have a fifty-fifty chance of their attempting to commit suicide before the age of twenty?

What country passed a law providing for at least five years in prison for trafficking in 500g of cocaine powder, and the same penalty for just 5g of "crack" cocaine?

What country has blacks comprising 82% of all "crack" cocaine offenders?

What country is considering reducing, retroactively, in 2007, the prison penalties for cocaine offenders, that would mean the early release of some 19,500 inmates?

What country was aided by France in its fight against Britain for independence, and actually had more French soldiers than Americans in the battle of Yorktown?

What country had a state legislature that had "wooden legs" as its largest expenditure during the first year after the Civil war?

What country has used burning at the stake, electric chairs, lethal injections, firing squads, gas chambers, and hangings to execute prisoners convicted of serious crimes?

What country has two states that prohibit veterinarians from using a particular drug when putting animals down, but it is still used by many other states when executing prison inmates?

What country has developed a mine-resistant, ambush-protected (MSAP) vehicle that costs $900,000 per unit, and has okayed the purchase of 15,000 of them by 2010?

What country has a "No Child Left Behind" law that mandates that all students become proficient in reading and math by 2014?

What country has over 4,500 schools serving over 2,000,000 children that have failed to bring enough students to grade level for four years, in 2007, making them subject to take "corrective action" under the "No Child Left Behind" law?

What country was on the losing end of a 184 to 4 vote in the United Nations General Assembly, urging them to end the forty-six year-old trade embargo of a tiny offshore island?

What country had a top Elder in the Mormon church say that they have over 3,000 churches worldwide, and that they are open to the public, and the public is always welcome?

What country had over sixty police officers fatally shot in 2007?

What country has six out of every ten workers who are balancing both work and caregiving?

What country has cigarette smoking as their leading cause of home fires, and so twenty-two states have adopted laws that require only self-extinguishing cigarettes be sold, with violators subject to severe penalties?

What country has a state that has put a cap of 3,000 for those low-income older adults that can receive in-home longtime health care, and have other 17,000 on their waiting list?

What country has estimated that by the year 2030, 25% of all drivers will be over the age of sixty-five?

What country experiences more fatal car accidents by seniors than teens?

What country has one city in the desert that actually has a growing union population?

What country sacked a government financial official who predicted early in the Iraq/Afghan wars that it would cost in the neighborhood of $200,000,000,000, and yet in 2007 a total of

$804,000,000,000 has been appropriated and the wars are still ongoing?

What country was a part of the victorious nations after WWI that demanded Germany pay war reparations amounting to $400,000,000,000 in today's dollars?

What country has discovered a relatively new dangerous infection called MRSA that is proving to be resistant to the penicillin-type antibiotics and has found its way into schools, fire stations and football teams, evidently through close contact between individuals?

What country in 2007 is building or planning to build 160 coal power plants and if they are all completed, the coal-plant emissions of carbon dioxide will rise 50%, along with noxious pollutants like sulfur dioxide, mercury and soot?

What country has a state where in 2007, one in every thirty-one homes is in foreclosure?

What country spent $8,000,000,000 on fuel for the Air Force during 2006?

What country has a wealthy man worth over $52,000,000,000 who says that wealthy people are not taxed enough?

What country has veterans from the Iraq war who are committing suicide at a rate of 120 per week?

What country that has serial killers and brutal murderers and rapists on the loose, put a man on the ''ten most wanted'' list who allegedly arranged for weddings of underage females in his church?

What country has an athlete who had a contract worth $41,000,000 to model underwear?

What country had a house burglar try to leave a home through the garage door, but it was broken so he then tried to go back through the door, but it had locked . . . the homeowners were on vacation, so he had to stay there for eight days subsisting only on a case of soda . . . he sued and was awarded $500,000 by the jury?

What country had a woman purchase a 32' motor home, and on her first trip she proceeded to set the cruise control at 70 miles per hour and went to the rear to make herself a sandwich . . . after the accident she sued and was awarded $1,750,000?

What country experienced over 1,000,000 cases of the sexually transmitted disease chlamydia, and over 350,000 cases of gonorrhea in 2006?

What country in 2004 had the percentage of black children in foster care over twice that of black children in the general population?

What country discovered in 2007 that some 30,000 doctors and other Medicaid providers owe federal taxes of over $1,000,000,000?

What country has over 6,000 planes in the air pretty much every day?

What country has just 40% of its people who go to church regularly, but 70% who want a president with strong religious faith?

What country has 75% of its processed foods contain one or more genetically modified ingredients?

What country witnessed Honda and Nissan going along with new legislation to increase fuel economy by 2020 and Toyota in opposition?

What country has one state that accounts for over one-half of all executions?

What country has just thirty-eight states that allow capital punishment?

What country discovered a manual that was used by city prosecutors of a large western city that stated, ''Do not take Jews, Negroes, Dagos, Mexicans, or a member of any minority race, on a jury, no matter how rich or well educated''?

What country has found that blacks are twice as likely than whites to have a stroke?

What country did not allow women to vote in 1872, and also did not allow them to be served alone in a restaurant after 6 P.M.?

What country in 2007 has had the value of its dollar against a Euro lose nearly 80% of its value since the year 2000?

What country had a study that determined that some 196,000 veterans slept on the street, in shelters, or in transitional housing in 2006?

What country in 2007 had seventy-four women in their House of Representatives and sixteen in the Senate?

What country has a woman who runs a network of some 5,500,000 people, most of them independent sales representatives for Avon products?

What country has an ID theft problem that costs the average victim $535 in out-of-pocket money, in addition to about twenty-five hours of time?

What country had 3,461 incidents of guns in schools between 2000 and 2004, and 10,970 incidents involving knives?

What country lost 320,000,000 large trees that were left flattened and rotting by the hurricane named Katrina?

What country turned away 200,000 people at the 326 legal air, sea and land entry points in 2006, out of the 400,000,000 who entered the country legally?

What country has estimated that about 21,000 people get into the country at legal entry points, who should not have been admitted, yearly?

What country has women traveling to India to have surrogate mothers have their children?

What country loses some 53,000,000 trees that are used just to make their yearly distribution of catalogs?

What country basically cut off most all immigration in 1924, and opened it up some in 1965 with a new immigration act?

What country mails out 20,000,000,000 catalogues yearly and over 98% are never looked at and end up in the trash?

What state attempted to "redirect" $600,000,000 of federal funds intended for homes for the victims of the hurricane Katrina, to the expansion of their ports?

What country has over 1,000,000 firefighters of whom 72% are volunteers?

What country came in thirty-third among countries that were ranked on the basis of gender equality, just one above Kazakhstan, by the Swiss-backed World Economic Forum?

What country has North Dakota leading in beer consumption per person, with Utah coming in last?

What country has experienced some 150 deaths after people were subdued by a stun gun?

What country can move a ton of freight 427 miles on one gallon of fuel, by train?

What country's law guarantees just twelve weeks of unpaid leave to new mothers, the least of any industrialized countries, some of which provide for a full year of paid leave?

What country has a large city that has experienced twenty-seven floods over the years and people continue to rebuild after each one?

What country has tried and convicted many people using bullet-lead analysis by the FBI for forty years, only to learn later that the science is severely flawed and is now considered "junk science"?

What country phased lead out of its gasoline beginning in 1973, and from residential house paint in 1978, along with lead-laden paint on toys?

What country tips an estimated $26,000,000,000 in 2006?

What country has almost half of its citizens who are over forty-five years old who do not have wills?

What country has 40% of all entitlement dollars such as Social Security, Medicaid, and Medicare, going to people under the age of 65?

What country has just half of its workers who participate in any retirement plan?

What country had a city that paid a PR firm $60,000 to help counter its image as the "most average" city in the country?

What country has more than 90% of its people who own a Bible, but just half can name a single Gospel?

What country has its average citizens living thirteen years longer than the average celebrity, who is four times as likely to commit suicide?

What country had its fathers spending 153% more time with their children in 2007 than they did in 1965?

What country has 242,000,000 of its 303,000,000 people living in a city or a suburb?

What country ranks just fortieth in the world in alcohol consumption per person?

What country ranks 107th among other world countries for savings rate?

What country ranks number one in the world in competitiveness, but is followed closely by Denmark and Sweden who have the highest tax burdens in the capitalist world, along with free education and health care and four years of unemployment benefits that amount to 90% of earnings?

What country had a city where 130 people were killed in 2006 by the use of guns, where just the possession of a handgun is illegal?

What country has potato chip makers that tell us it takes four pounds of potatoes to make one pound of potato chips?

What country has a murder rate nearly five times that of Italy?

What country has 1,023 vehicles for every 1,000 people over sixteen years of age, compared to China with nine vehicles for everyone over sixteen?

What country had a woman who signed a $500,000,000 deal with K-Mart?

What country had a woman who was worth maybe $1,000,000,000 who went to prison for essentially trying to avoid a loss of about $45,000 in the stock market?

What country would have ever predicted that Martha Stewart and Michael Vick would serve time in prison, while O.J. Simpson was out playing golf?

What country now has so-called "presidential physical exams" that go for $1400 and more?

What country has gays and lesbians accounting for some $55,000,000,000 of the country's travel market?

What country's veterans are coming back from the Afghan and Iraq war to find that the scaled-down GI bill is only paying about one-tenth of their university and housing fees, and many will leave college with student loan debts of around $60,000?

What country had 8,000,000 WWII veterans who took advantage of the educational GI bill after the end of the war, and got college educations or vocational training on the government's dime?

What country's Pentagon testified in 2007 that the newly proposed increases to the existing GI bill would actually HURT the military because it would attract new recruits, but that "retaining" them would be more difficult because many would go on to college after their first term, and leave the military?

What country is the only major country in the world in 2007 that was experiencing a tourist travel decline in the midst of a global boom?

What country experienced, between 2000 and 2006, a drop of over 10% in Britons visiting their country at the same time British travel to Turkey was up by 82%, to India was up by 102%, and to New Zealand up by 106%?

What country, ever since 9/11, has had the alert level at "elevated" or above 5 and even higher at airports?

What country had a study of 534 same-sex twins and determined that "Twins who had sex earlier had lower levels of delinquency, and anti-social behavior a few tears later, not more"?

What country has a national average of teens having sex at age sixteen?

What country witnessed a surge in home mortgage defaults between 2005 and 2007 of 75%?

What country has libraries now that loan out "e-books" that evaporate at the end of the loan period?

What country's mortgage loan industry made so-called "exploding" loans at, say 7% for the first few years, that jumped to 10% or even 15%, after that?

What country discovered in 2007 that the share of the nation's income going to the top one percent is at its highest in eighty years?

What country's federal government in 2007 provided about half of the millions of pounds of food they previously provided to large cities for the poor?

What country had a politician slip a change into a college education financial aid bill that kids of owners of small businesses of less than 100 employees would not be subject to the strict limits of finances ... the only problem is that 98% of the nation's 5,800,000 businesses have less than ninety-nine employees?

What country had a president who, by late 2007, had made 167 "recess appointments" to important federal government jobs while Congress was not in session, to avoid the normal Congressional confirmation process?

What country had a fifteen-year-old pitch in a major league baseball game, in 1944?

What country has just 6% of its workforce that makes over $97,000 per year?

What country is considering removing the cap of $97,000 for paying social security taxes, that would require higher income people to continue to pay into social security after their income exceeds $97,000, and it would increase revenues by some $122,000,000,000 per year?

What country is evaluating some 2,000 colonels to determine who will become one-star generals, in 2007?

What country was recently reminded of an overseas cyclone in 1970 that was responsible for the deaths of 500,000 people?

What country sold 3,000,000 GPS devices in 2006 and an estimated 8,000,000 in 2007?

What country had an auto company that invested some $1,000,000,000 during the 1990s in an attempt to build an electrical vehicle, but found it was too expensive, took too long to charge, and had no backup engine?

What country has an auto company in 2007 that was close to coming up with a car with a T-shaped battery that will have an exceptional takeoff speed, will be quieter, and charging from a power outlet will be about 80% less than gas would be at $3.00 per gallon?

What country has some 20,000,000 people with type-2 diabetes, and is estimated to have 48,000,000 by the year 2050?

What country had a president in the 60s who poured tens of thousands of soldiers into the Viet Nam War, at the same time his personal conversations revealed that he had grave doubts about the war?

What country is a part of the occupation of Afghanistan, and has witnessed the production of 8,200 tons of opium in the sixth year after the invasion?

What country is still trying in 2007 to help bring together the Jews and the Arabs when the average income of an Arab in Jerusalem is $4,000 per compared to $19,000 for a Jew?

What country has some 83,000,000 of its people visiting the internet's social networking sites monthly?

What country has an internet operation named "Google" that is valued at about $200,000,000,000?

What country has belatedly discovered that giving over-the-counter cold medicines to children under six years of age is more harmful than helpful?

What country has women suffering from migraine headaches three times the rate as men?

What country has learned that smoking one marijuana cigarette has the same effect on the lungs as smoking five cigarettes in succession?

What country has discovered that newly married men and women age eighteen to twenty-eight gain an average of up to nine pounds more than their single peers?

What country has estimated that the population of amputees will increase by 42% by the year 2020, partly due to returning veterans of the Iraq war?

What country has an estimated 14% who profess to have no religion, and that percentage rises to 20% for eighteen to twenty-five year-olds?

What country's clothes dryers contribute up to a ton of CO_2 per household per year, and use up to 6% of total electricity?

What country has some communities that have banned the use of environmentally friendly clotheslines because they are eyesores?

What country might have more regulations pertaining to toy guns, than real guns?

What country has its nation's capitol city with the highest rate of HIV of any other city in the country?

What country has a religious cult that pickets funerals of soldiers killed in Iraq with signs saying things like ''GOD HATES FAGS!'' and was ordered by a judge to pay $11,000,000 in damages to the family of a Marine that sued them?

What country has a former mayor of a huge city, who is running for President in 2007, whose father was a strongarm man for his brother-in-law and ended up in Sing Sing prison for a year, for mugging a milkman?

What country proposed ''Roadmap'' for peace in the Middle East, that prohibited the expansion of settlements in the West Bank, but then stood by as that provision was ignored and the population of settlements grew by 20% at the same time the Israeli population grew just almost 2%?

What country had a woman who lobbied 5 different Presidents before she was able to convince President Lincoln in 1863 to declare the holiday known as Thanksgiving?

What country has a state that is proposing a law patterned after 19 other countries including Sweden, Israel and Britain, that outlaws parents from spanking their children, with a penalty of jail time?

What country has gone from providing 2,000,000 CT scans in 1980 to some 62,000,000 in 2007?

What country is warning their people that CT scans have 100 to 200 times the radiation that you get from a normal X-ray, and should be used sparingly?

What country has a gift tax law that requires a person who accepts a gift worth over $10,000, to must pay taxes on that gift?

What country in 2007 has an immigrant population of 37,900,000 considered both legal and illegal?

What country had immigrants accounting for one resident in twenty-one in 1970, one in sixteen in 1980, one in thirteen in 1990 and one in eight in 2007?

What country has had 10,300,000 immigrants arriving between 2000 and 2007?

What country had a mother of a soldier collect 80,000 cans of Silly String to be used in Iraq and Afghanistan for squirting across rooms to help detect any trip wire explosives by watching it as it falls?

What country's soldiers use cigarette butts and condoms to cover the open end of the barrels of their rifles to keep the sand out?

What country allows the videotaping in department stores of customers undressing in changing rooms, in most states?

What country has a minister who is famous for saying, "Before marriage, opposites attract. After marriage, opposites attack?"

What country had a former mayor of a huge city who earned $11,400,000 in speaking fees between January 2006 and May of 2007?

What country's tax payers are financing the return of Iraqi people who are moving back from other countries in 2007, to the tune of $750 to ease their "transition"?

What country has had over 169 murders in its capital city in the year 2007?

What country has opened fewer embassies in Africa than China?

What country loses about 25,000 children under the age of ten yearly, due to things like car accidents, congenital anomalies, premature birth, cancer, and other unintentional injuries?

What country has allowable income tax deductions of up to $500 for certain energy-saving actions in 2007?

What country had a vice presidential candidate in 2004 who not only lost the vote in his home state, but his congressional district too, and even his own precinct?

What country had a woman convicted of murdering her son and sent to prison for it, has petitioned for continuing to receive alimony checks from her former husband when she is released from prison, and the court agreed?

What country had a 25 mpg average fuel consumption imposed upon vehicle manufacturers in 2007 while China was averaging 30 mpg, Europe 37 and Japan 40?

What country's scientists no longer believe that eggs have a significant impact on blood cholesterol?

What country seized a record 14,000 shipments of counterfeit "knockoff" products coming into the country in 2006?

What country has an estimated $250,000,000,000 loss in sales to legitimate businesses, due to counterfeit products?

What country had a woman who was paying $650 per month for health insurance when she was diagnosed with breast cancer, and the insurance company paid for the surgery and a three-day stay in the hospital, but $100,000 worth of other related expenses were not covered?

What country had a man who paid an insurance company $25 per month for coverage in 1980, had his premiums raised yearly until it reached his latest renewal cost of $4,284 per month in 2007?

What country had a drug company that spent $52,000,000 in one twelve-month period advertising a new diabetes drug, when older drugs that cost much less were equally effective?

What country has about 40% of its people who return at least one Christmas present after the holidays?

What country has a former ambassador to the United Nations who said if military force was ever used against Iran, that the nation would have to "make it clear to the people of Iran that it is not aimed against them?"

What country has 3,900,000 pigeons in one of its largest cities, and is considering imposing a $1,000 fine for anyone who feeds them?

What country had a survey conducted by the nonpartisan Urban Institute that concluded that immigrants in one state paid more in Social Security and sales taxes than they cost in social services like health care and education?

What country's Navy unleashed an artillery barrage on northern Somalia, on June 1, 2007, that killed many, but went largely unreported in the nation's media?

What country's household debt was 55% of income in 1983, and was 114% in 2007?

What country's schoolgirls suffered over 29,000 concussions from playing soccer between 2005 and 2006, and 13,000 from playing basketball?

What country eliminated a century-old ban on the sale of absinthe, and in 2007 allowed two European distillers to sell it at a price per bottle of about $50 to $60 each?

What country has an organization called "Engineers without Borders," that designed a pump that supplies water to remote communities in the developing world without using electricity?

What country has guarded the Tomb of the Unknown Soldier twenty-four hours a day, seven days a week ever since 1930 . . . its guards take about five hours to prepare, assemble and put on their uniforms and they are replaced every thirty minutes?

What country had a national debt of over $9,130,000,000,000 increasing at a rate of $1,000,000 per minute in 2007?

What country had a national debt that is equal to over $30,000 for every man, woman and child in the nation in 2007?

What country lost some 600 food inspectors working for the FDA between 2003 and 2007, mostly due to cuts in funds by Congress?

What country has a state that is planning to build a super highway 1,200 feet wide, to accommodate vehicles, trains, water lines, electricity, etc., that will require some 500,000 acres to be taken by eminent domain, and will cost the state some $180,000,000,000, with construction scheduled to begin in 2009?

What country has health spending that totals some $2,000,000,000,000, and is expected to almost double by 2030?

What country has companies spending about $9,000 yearly for an employee family health insurance policy?

What country has black males ages fifteen to nineteen who die by homicide at forty-six times the rate of white males their age?

What country has about 6,000,000 couples who have infertility problems?

What country has over half of the uninsured making under $30,000 per year, and are unable to afford a typical family health insurance policy that costs $10,000 or more per year?

What country admitted nearly 500,000 people to a hospital due to osteoporosis-related fractures, in 2007?

What country permitted Israel to move settlers into occupied land following the 1967 war, against international law, and four decades later finds it an irresolvable problem preventing peace in the Middle East?

What country is beginning to have police substations inside its malls?

What country's people save and invest less than 2% of their income, while in China the rate is over 35%?

What country took six Algerian men who had been released in Bosnia by that nation's highest court, and brought them to Guantanamo where they have been for over six years without trial?

What country had released over half of the original 770 Guantanamo detainees, without charges, by 2007?

What country has witnessed six Republican Senators declare that they will retire from government, along with 17 Republican members of the House Representatives, in 2007?

What country was the only large industrialized nation still holding out in 2007 for signing the Kyoto protocol, since Australia's newly elected president has vowed to sign up?

What country has its capital city with about one in every forty residents who have HIV or AIDS, compared to the nation's average of one in every 779?

What country has issued state coin quarters that have generated some $4,000,000,000 in profits to the Treasury?

What country passed a law in 1984 that required companies to file detailed reports if they stored or released more than 500 pounds of toxins, only to have the EPA in 2007 change it to 5,000 pounds?

What country initiated ''Project Camelot'' where anthropologists were sent to Chile and concealed their military assignment to research the potential for an internal war there?

What country has nearly 6,000 teens who die in car crashes every year?

What country had high school dropouts earning about $20,000 per year in 2005, while someone with a bachelor's degree makes $54,000?

What country has witnessed the eradication of smallpox, a disease that was responsible for the deaths of 500,000,000 people worldwide in the 20th century?

What country witnessed 945 Israelis murdered during the decade following the Oslo ''peace'' agreement, whereas the decade prior to it saw just forty-one murdered?

What country had over 7,000,000 people in prisons and jails, or on parole or probation, or under some court supervision, in 2007?

What country routinely creates between 2 million and 3 million jobs per month, and also destroys somewhere between 2 and 3 million jobs?

What country hired 1,800 new air traffic controllers in 2006, and by late 2007 only forty were ready for taking on the job of controlling aircraft?

What country had 170,000 people with their homes in foreclosure in 2007?

What country spent $123,000,000 on red hair dye in 2006?

What country had thirty-six deaths attributed directly to football in 1968?

What country had 12,000,000 immigrants go through Ellis Island in 1939 who were screened for disease and mental illnesses?

What country had its first automobile built by Henry Ford, built to run on alcohol, and not gasoline?

What country had the murder rate by young black men increase by 70% between the years 2002 to 2007?

What country has had just three women awarded the Nobel Peace Prize?

What country handed out 8,000,000 passports in 2004 and 18,000,000 in 2007?

What country experiences about $60,000,000,000 worth of fraud related to medicare, yearly?

What country had a convicted murderer who was about to be released from prison, when officials discovered a shoelace in his cell and a prosecutor convinced a jury that it was a "deadly weapon," and he was sentenced to 20 to 40 more years in prison?

What country had a proposed amendment to its constitution that would have declared the nation's dependence on, and allegiance to, Jesus, and it was buried by President Lincoln?

What country's congress set aside $75,000,000 in 2006 to "promote democracy" in Iran?

What country has had fourteen Russian children killed by their adoptive parents since the early 1990s?

What country had eighty-one children adopted from overseas countries that were ultimately relinquished to officials in fourteen states, in 2006?

What country had 180,000,000 prescriptions for reducing cholesterol filled in 2006?

What country has what amounts to "socialized medicine" for some 5,000,000 veterans?

What country has some 700 military bases overseas?

What country has a first lady who posed with the president for some 120,000 photos during the first seven years of his presidency?

What country had about sixty potential performance-enhancing drugs available to athletes, and yet Major League Baseball just test for thirty of them and the NFL just tested for ten in 2007?

What country had a sitting president publicly declare that he "loathed" the leader of another country in the Far East, in 2002?

What country has six ministers in its Congress in 2007?

What country had some 6,000,000 "extra" households in 2007, because of broken marriages . . . up from 1,400,000 in

1970, resulting in about $10,600,000,000 per year inefficiencies in electricity and water consumption?

What country released 169,000 prison inmates in 1980 from state and federal custody, and almost 700,000 in 2005?

What country found that 8,000 of its new Army recruits in 2006 had criminal records, and had to be granted waivers to allow them to join?

What country has installed some automated ''probation kiosks'' that resemble ATMs where offenders must scan their hands and respond to basic questions for about three minutes?

What country tracks some 17,300 objects in space, including debris from an aging weather satellite that was blown up by the Chinese in 2007?

What country had 400 satellites in space, in 2007?

What country had the stock of an internet company go from its initial offering price of $85 a share in 2004, to $740 in 2007?

What country's teenagers ranked behind Slovenia and Estonia, among others, in science and math in 2007?

What country has a White House that sent out 895,000 Christmas cards in 2007?

What country gives automatic citizenship to an estimated 350,000 babies born to illegal immigrants yearly?

What country's ''Habitat for Humanity'' built some 200,000 homes over a thirty-year period for poor people?

What country has an estimated 65,000 service men and women serving in the military under the so-called ''Don't ask, don't tell'' policy in 2007?

What country has paid a civilian ''tipster'' $225,000 to record conversations between him and an ice-cream-truck driver and his son, in an effort to determine if they were dangerous potential terrorists?

What country reduced the top tax rate from 70% to 28% during one president's eight years in office?

What country had a sitting President who publicly called a country of over 300,000,000 people, an "Evil Empire"?

What country has three states that in 2007 began random drug testing of their high school athletes to detect steroid use?

What country has one state where the "safe haven" law includes children who are up to one year old that can be dropped off at approved places without any penalty to the mother?

What country allows professional telephone fund raisers to keep up to 95% of what they raise?

What country finds that fares for a transatlantic cruise on Queen Mary II go from $1,500 up to $30,000?

What country has a large National Park that has some 20,000 elk, 3000 wolves, and over 200 lakes?

What country solved about 85% of its murders in the 1970s, but only about 50% in the early 21st century?

What country loses an average of thirty to forty babies per year when they are left in enclosed cars in hot weather?

What country in 2006 lowered mental and physical standards, doubled enlistment bonuses, tripled reenlistment bonuses, and gave waivers to convicted felons, to meet its military enlistment goals?

What country's historic buffs were surprised to learn that the mighty 300 Spartan warriors were mostly homosexuals?

What country has a department store that is offering a $215,000 bottle of perfume?

What country had an Iraqi judge estimate that some $18,000,000,000 of government money has disappeared between 2003 and 2007?

What country had a B-52 bomber "accidentally" loaded with six nuclear weapons, and flown from one state to another, that went unnoticed for over thirty-six hours?

What country's astronomers witnessed the explosion of a star that was estimated to be 100 to 200 times the size of the sun, and about 240 million light-years away?

212

What country has a package delivery company that started in 1973 by delivering 183 packages on its first day of business, and in 2007 has 75,000 trucks, 669 jets and is handling up to 11,000,000 packages daily?

What country had a Wall Street firm that paid its employees in 2007 $20,200,000,000 in salaries, options and bonuses, and that amounts to an average of $661,000 per employee?

What country had no income tax prior to 1913?

What country gives three times the foreign aid to Arab countries as it does to Israel?

What country has almost one-third of all breast-augmentation done on patients who are women age forty and over?

What country had sales of 125,000 tasers to the public over a ten-year period?

What country's Sentencing Commission unanimously agreed that almost 20,000 federal inmates convicted of ''crack'' possession, could apply for sentence reductions in 2007?

What country has just 7% of federal cocaine cases directed at high-level traffickers?

What country had its Electoral College called ''the most dangerous blot on our Constitution'' by Thomas Jefferson?

What country passed legislation in 2004 that provided that victims of crimes must be allowed to speak during bail and sentencing hearings?

What country has estimated that just 7% of court-ordered restitution payments are actually collected, and federal criminal debt stood at over $46,000,000,000 in 2006?

What country passed an alternative minimum tax bill in 1969 that was intended to prevent millionaires from avoiding income tax altogether?

What country provided 340,000 pounds of Christmas turkeys to GIs in the Italian front during WWII?

What country had some 26,000 troops in Afghanistan while NATO had about 28,000, in 2007?

What country has expelled 22,500 soldiers from the service, between 2003 and 2007, for ''personality disorders''?

What country experienced a mild explosion of cell phones, while India was signing up 8,000,000 more cell phone users every month, in 2007?

What country imports more oil from Canada than it does from Saudi Arabia?

What country had a school board in one northeastern state that approved providing eleven-year-old girls with birth control pills?

What country provided Afghans over $1,000,000,000 worth of Stinger missiles and other military hardware to use in their war against the USSR in the 1980s?

What country has the crime of animal cruelty as a felony in 43 states?

What country has a military presence in 130 countries and about 700 bases?

What country had 572,000 troops based overseas in 2007?

What country had a quarterback who was selected in the sixth round of the NFL draft, the 199th player, come to win three Super Bowls and sign a contract worth some $60,000,000 just a few years later?

What country has a genetic genealogy company that specializes in DNA, finding that one-third of their black male clients have a white male relative somewhere back in time?

What country has determined that if you go back twenty generations, you will have over 1,000,000 grandparents?

What country has 90% of its population that believes in God, but just 25% go to church every week?

What country provided target information to Turkey that allowed the Turkish air force to launch air strikes into Northern Iraq, in late 2007?

What country's Environmental Protection Agency has estimated that it produces 2,600,000 tons of electronic waste from products such as discarded TVs and computers, yearly?

What country sends about 132,000 tons of electronic waste from items such as computers and TVs, to China and India, yearly, to be picked over and tiny bits of copper and gold, salvaged?

What country has determined that Saudi Arabia has taken in over $800,000,000,000 of oil wealth in the past five years?

What country is the second largest consumer of oil consumption per capita, with Saudi Arabia being at the top?

What country, for the first time, in 2006, has cell phone households, outnumbering land-line-only ones?

What country has passed a law that phases out the use of the ordinary incandescent bulbs by 2012?

What country consumed nearly 30,000,000,000 bottles of bottled water in 2007?

What country belongs to the so-called western world, where a child uses thirty times the resources as a child born in a third-world country?

What country was investigating, in 2007, its own military and also civilian contractors to determine if they were involved in the disappearance of 110,000 AK-47 rifles and 80,000 pistols that were intended for Iraqi security forces?

What country experienced a huge fire in 2007 that covered over 500,000 acres and was fought by 10,000 people, including 3,000 convicts, firefighters, its military, and firefighters from Mexico?

What country has never had a millionaire on death row, and people who say that will never happen?

What country had 18,000 owners of ATVs in one western state, and 118,000 five years later?

What country has Ronald McDonald as the second-most recognized character in the world, following just Santa Claus?

What country has the power window of places like fast food drive-ins, as their fastest growing appliance?

What country had french fries potatoes introduced to it by Thomas Jefferson, after his ambassadorship to France?

What country had a ''Big Mac'' invented in 1967 that went on to sell over 550,000,000 in its home country alone?

What country has the tomato as its most popular fruit, followed by the banana?

What country has a fast food franchise that in 2007 had over 31,000 locations in over 100 countries that served over 50,000,000 customers?

What country has had just two black Senators and three black Governors since the days of reconstruction?

What country has 400 stores that sell legal medical marijuana in just the southern part of one Western state?

What country has a dozen states that have legalized medical marijuana?

What country had 9,000,000 acres burnt by fires in 2007?

What country has had seven of the top ten biggest fire seasons between 1999 and 2007?

What country has one popular movie star who has been in and out of rehab eight times?

What country raised one turkey in 2007 for nearly every person?

What country has males committing 93% of its murders?

What country has more police officers killed during traffic stops than in any other way?

What country had the lowest total number of airplane crashes since 1963, in 2007?

What country took fifty years to give women the right to vote, after giving black men that right?

What country had one airport that had over 1,000,000 flights coming and going in 2007?

What country lost over 5,000 helicopters during the Viet Nam War?

What country has a city that averages 128 inches of rain yearly?

What country has just 17,000,000 people who buy their own health insurance?

What country has watched as China has been responsible for about 75% of the reduction of poverty over the past century?

What country has some fast trains, but nothing that compares to the 268 MPH magnetic-levitation train that runs between Shanghai and its airport?

What country's evening network news shows draw just about 10% of the viewing audience?

What country's capital city spends more per public school student than almost every other major school district, but have some of the worst test scores in the country?

What country's insurance companies will pay for an expensive operation to amputate the foot of a diabetic, but will not pay for cheaper preventive visits to a podiatrist that could make surgery unnecessary?

What country's seven out of the last ten elections have been won with less than 51% of the vote?

What country quarantined its first person in 2007, since the last one was in 1963?

What country had to laugh when informed that Britain's National Health Service told a woman she would have to wait 18 months to get her hearing aid, despite the fact that she was 108 years old?

What country saw a rise in people who say they don't believe in God, from 2% in 2001 to 6% in 2007?

What country's leading cause of death among pregnant women . . . is murder?

What country experiences more collect phone calls on Father's Day than any other day of the year?

What country has an average cost of raising a medium size dog until age 11, at $16,400?

What country has about 61,000 people airborne at any given hour?

What country has about 38% of its land as wilderness, while Africa has just about 28%?

What country's original color of Coke, was green?

What country prints more Monopoly money daily, than the federal treasure does?

What country had a billionaire who offered $1,000,000 cash to any of the richest 400 men if they could show that they paid a higher rate of income taxes than their secretaries, and none took him up on it?

What country's fitness clubs experience a 60% increase in business every January?

What country has 300,000 pregnant women who are abused by their partners yearly?

What country had 1,300 pregnant women murdered between 1990 and 2004?

What country issued a 24¢ stamp that was upside-down and later sold to a collector for $825,000?

What country is increasingly using billboards to show photos of wanted criminals?

What country's recording industry is prosecuting a man for transferring legally purchased music on a CD, onto his personal computer, in 2007?

What country subsidizes an airline $1,343 for each round trip it makes between Lewiston and Billings, Montana . . . a route that averaged just two passengers a day in 2006?

What country carries out fewer than three in 100 death sentences that are imposed in any given year?

What country has a state where there are fifty-five prison inmates who have been on death row for over twenty-five years?

What country had the Supreme Court Justice who cast the deciding vote that "saved" capital punishment in 1987, say in his biography that that was the vote that he most regretted?

What country has no universal health care for its people, yet found $21,000,000,000 to provide to Pakistan between 1954 and 2007?

What country made a hero out of a former female Pakistan leader in 2007, despite the fact that Amnesty International accused her government of having one of the worst records of custodial deaths, killings and torture, and she was also accused of having laundered $1,500,000,000 through Swiss banks while in office?

What country had an NFL football team go unbeaten through the 2007 regular season with a team payroll of about $118,000,000 equaling the unbeaten record of a 1972 team that did it with a payroll of about $1,500,000?

What country's Social Security system will see its rolls boosted from some 50,000,000 to 80,000,000 over the next two decades?

What country has a Social Security system where all age groups since 1937 have put in more into it than they got out of it?

What country's fishermen envy those in Japan where a single blue fin tuna can bring in as much as $20,000?

What country's consumers make up 70% of the nation's economic activity?

What country, for the first time since the 19th century, saw the average British citizen earn $500 more than his or her counterpart in 2007?

What country had a political party boss travel over 528,000 air miles over a period of almost three years, not counting any of his international flights?

What country had at least some 42,000,000 abortions performed between 1973 and 2002?

What country has had the number of vehicles entering the downtown section of a large city, grow annually by an average of 8,000 per day since the 1920s?

What country has an estimated gaming market of $56,000,000,000 per year, while its most famous gambling city does less than $7,000,000,000?

What country has a senator who is asking Congress to provide $250,000,000,000 to rebuild a flood devastated city . . . that would mean $516,528 for every man, woman and child resident?

What country is experiencing a rash of catalytic converter thefts from autos and trucks because of the existence of a few grams of platinum in them since the price of platinum rising to about $1,500 per ounce?

What country had a study in 2007 that revealed the average woman uses 7,000 words a day and the average man, just 2,000?

What country ranked dead last in a 2007 survey of 19 industrialized countries for preventable deaths before the age of 75?

What country has some 90,000,000 of its people who suffer from some form of chronic illnesses?

What country is beginning to install cellular routers and rooftop antennas to school busses so kids can have high-speed internet access during ninety-minute rides to and from school?

What country has some 3,500,000 students who are opting for online college courses?

What country has some politicians who are suggesting a system like the Danes have whereby the government pays workers who have lost their jobs almost their entire salary while they look for new employment?

What country had a Secretary of the Interior in the 1920s who accepted $400,000 in cash and gifts from oil barons of the day?

What country is exporting high-tech jobs to India where professional rat-catchers who can catch up to twenty rats per day, will earn a total of $1?

What country had one state that passed a law requiring the ninety-day suspension of driver's licenses for anyone under eighteen who is caught speeding?

What country has estimated that the polar bear population of the world could be reduced by two-thirds over the next fifty years due to further Arctic ice melt?

What country had one midwestern state that experienced 18,000 homes that were disconnected from utilities at the beginning of the 2007 winter?

What country has noted that scientists tracked one leatherback turtle who swam 12,774 miles in 674 days?

What country had some 97,000 people waiting for organs for transplanting in 2007?

What country had police arrest a high school student after checking ''Facebook'' web site photos on the internet, showing him in possession of alcohol?

What country has a leather belt that sells for $18,000, due mainly to its having a platinum buckle?

What country in 2007, finds the typical household spending $1,300 more per year on gasoline, than in 2002?

What country's airport inspectors find an average of two guns per day at airports throughout the country?

What country has Kentucky Fried Chicken and Pizza Hut restaurants in some 12,000 locations in 110 countries?

What country has Taco Bell planning to expand 300 of their restaurants into Mexico?

What country experienced nine recessions from 1942 to 1982?

What country has an $800 baby stroller on the market that is selling well?

What country has a state that has more ''payday loan'' lenders that can charge up to 36% interest plus ''fees'', than Starbucks and McDonald's combined?

What country had AARP members go from 100,000 in 1958 to over 39,000,000 in 2007?

What country had just 8% of the people who filed income tax returns in 2006 who designated $3 of their taxes to public financing of the presidential campaigns, even though it would cost them nothing?

What country had some 35% of the voters in the 2004 election were those over fifty years old, and just two years later that figure was 52%?

What country had a president in 1938 who was told by a one-star general that his defense strategy was all wrong . . . and to the surprise of many, was made chief of staff of the Army?

What country, in addition to Russia was permitted to retain research samples of the smallpox virus, under closely monitored secure conditions, after it was eradicated in 1977?

What country has an estimated 40% of all undocumented immigrants who entered the country legally, and overstayed their visas?

What country had their banks in thirty-three of the forty-eight states closed in the spring of 1933, and unemployment rampant?

What country's delegation was told to "Lead, follow, or get out of the way" by Papua New Guinea, in Bali, during a conference on global warming?

What country pays Sunnis in Iraq, who are former insurgents, about $300 per month in return for their cooperation?

What country has one of the highest rates of caesareans and of infant mortality?

What country finds that caesarean risk of death by the mothers is three times that of natural birth, and two times for the infant?

What country has 5,300,000 people who live with heart failure, a chronic condition that starves the heart of blood?

What country had cell phone only households numbering just 3% in 2003, to 13% in 2006 and about 25% in 2007?

What country was once admired by most Turks, but has fallen to a 9% favorable opinion in 2007?

What country's presidential election in 1960 was run on the promise to "close the missile gap" with the Soviet Union, only to learn later that it had some 2,000 missiles to the USSR's 67?

What country, in the 1800 presidential election, had a newspaper that favored John Adams, declaring that if Thomas Jefferson should win, then "murder, robbery, rape, adultery, and incest will all be openly taught and practiced."

What country had a man pour $4,500,000 of his own resources into the organization responsible for the "Swift Boat" campaign in the 2004 presidential election?

What country had a presidential candidate in 1828 who eventually won, who was guilty of being married to a woman who was still married to another man?

What country had a presidential Bull Moose party candidate running in the early 1900s who was shot in the chest by a .32 caliber bullet, and yet insisted on addressing his audience, saying, "The bullet is in me now, so that I cannot make a very long speech"?

What country, in 1824, had the House of Representatives choose the President, after none of the candidates won enough electoral votes to claim victory?

What country was dominated by one political party in 1824 called the Democratic-Republican party, which split in two when Andrew Jackson and John Quincy Adams became rivals?

What country launched 4,719 new Kosher food items in 2007?

What country has one of its top universities that has an endowment fund of over $23,000,000,000?

What country's credit card companies have the right to change the terms of accounts at any time and for any reason, and have been known to double or triple interest rates for customers whose payment arrives one day late?

What country's average student debt for those graduating from a four-year public college in 2004 was $15,000 . . . up from $8,800 in 1993?

What country had an FBI agent interview Saddam Hussein for months after his capture and he revealed that the main reason Iraq invaded Kuwait was that the Emir of Kuwait insulted his emissary by saying he wished all "Iraqi women would turn into $10 prostitutes"?

What country launched some fifty air strikes specifically aimed at killing Saddam Hussein during the "Shock and Awe" portion of the Iraq war . . . without success?

What country had one real estate agent who sold 102 homes in one state in 2007, and all of them went into foreclosure?

What country had a popular funeral home that had been in business for over 100 years, bought by a new owner, who proceeded to advise his 13,500 customers who had prepaid funeral contracts, that they were invalid unless they paid an additional $3,500?

What country employed a record 67,000,000 women during 2007?

What country has a huge retail sales company that serves 100,000,000 customers every week?

What country has almost one-half of all fraudulent credit card use originate at restaurants when patrons hand their credit cards over to waiters and waitresses?

What country had a presidential candidate who in 2007 said that we should stay in Iraq for 100 years, if necessary?

What country has sold China over $400,000,000,000 worth of bonds?

What country had 350 attempted suicides of military personnel in 2002 and 2,100 in 2007?

What country had nearly 4,300,000 children born in 2007, the largest number since the years following the end of WWII?

What country has learned that ships account for twice as much global emissions as airplanes?

What country has the average health care per person spending of $6,000 per person per year, while countries like the Congo spend just $15?

What country had its unemployment inching up by 0.3% in 2007, resulting in 474,000 fewer people on payrolls?

What country's people spend some $9,000,000,000,000 while the combined yearly consumer spending of China and India accounts for just $1,600,000,000?

What country has a man running for President in 2007 who graduated near the bottom of his class at the Naval Academy, despite having an IQ of 131?

What country in 2007 had a person who earns $38,000 per year, and got a loan for a $700,000 home?

What country has a burglary taking place every fifteen seconds?

What country had 16,000,000 plastic surgery procedures performed in 2007?

What country has published a controversial book that reminds people that Jesus once said, ''Anyone who loves father or mother more than me, is not worthy of me''?

What country saw their international trade deficit shrink by $100,000,000,000 in 2007, but mainly due to the decline of the dollar?

What country conducted a survey of their citizens of all ages and found in them 148 chemicals, including lead, mercury, dioxins, and PCBs?

What country has more than 1,000,000 high school students who give up on their education every year?

What country had 13% of their eighteen to twenty-nine-year olds who paid attention to the presidential campaign in 2000, with that figure rising to 74% in 2008?

What country in 2008 discovered a new booming business where parties are thrown for a divorced person who is presented with gifts that include things such as voodoo dolls ready for the pins, and coffins for the wedding ring?

What country has more books about President Lincoln, than any other president?

What country elected President Lincoln after having served just one term as a Representative from Illinois, and found on his first full day in office, a letter from Fort Sumter's commander asking for 20,000 men?

What country has learned that President Lincoln's wife's family had slaves, and her two brothers fought on the side of the Confederacy?

What country uses discarded old car batteries for making most all lead bullets?

What country had 4,700,000 serve during WWII?

What country paid a so-called ''whistle blower'' over $60,000,000 for his role against a large pharmaceutical company's unlawful practices?

What large, reputable drug company paid $671,000,000 to settle claims that it overcharged Medicaid, and paid kickbacks to doctors?

What country is losing its auto manufacturing capability to countries like Canada where health costs associated with the production of each vehicle produced is about $800 versus Detroit, Michigan's $6,000?

What country had a conservative president take office with a national debt of about $5,000,000,000,000 and seven years later has a debt of over $9,000,000,000,000?

What country had a political party impose a $10 fine upon its members if they referred to their presidential opposition by the names ''Hillary'' or ''Barack'' . . . and their logic was that using their first names tended to make them sound more likable?

What country has some twenty-eight states that have passed legislation banning smoking in eating establishments?

What country had smoking among adults decline from 43% to 20% during the years 1965 to 2007?

What country had the department of health of one small state estimate that 1,700 deaths could be attributed to second-hand smoke?

What country has a median household income of over $48,000, and in some localities it's over $80,000?

What country lost over 3,000,000 manufacturing jobs between 1995 and 2005?

What country has just over 18% of those over 85, living in nursing homes?

What country has some 80,000,000 so-called baby boomers who will become eligible for Social Security benefits in the two decades following 2007?

What country has estimated that billing errors involving health insurance exceed $100,000,000,000 per year?

What country has learned that Interpol lists 30,000 stolen paintings and fewer than one in five are ever recovered?

What country has some 175,000,000 people who are paying 19% average interest on credit cards, on a total debt of $966,000,000,0000?

What country had a woman who advertised on internet's "craig's list" for a hit man to kill her lover's wife for $5,000?

What country had a presidential candidate who spent some $60,000,000 during the 2007 Republican primary, and ended up with one delegate?

What country's people spent over $2,000,000,000 in 2007 changing the ring tones on their cell phones?

What country has Mexican workers sending some $20,000,000,000 yearly to their families south of the border?

What country had over 2,000 people murdered during the five years preceding 2008, in the District of Columbia?

What country in 2008 had twelve states that have legalized medical marijuana?

What country in 2008 found that almost half of Russians believe that its objective is the complete destruction of Russia?

What country has more than twice as many people with mental illness who live in prisons as in mental institutions?

What country now has some 175 "mental health courts" where defendants are diverted to treatment programs instead of to jail or probation?

What country had discovered that Denmark is ranked as the happiest country in the world, and it has free health care, free college, subsidized child and elderly care, six weeks annual vacations, and taxes for the middle class that amount to about 50% of their income?

What country has a drug that was meant to control bleeding during surgery, that was given to some 400,000 patients during a period when studies showed it was dangerous, and it was estimated that the FDA could have saved 22,000 lives if it had been taken it off the market?

What country is a major player in auto manufacturing, but doesn't come close to the Chinese, who put over 2,000 new vehicles on their roads every day, in 2008?

What country had some 500,000 people in their mental institutions in 1955, and just about 50,000 in 2008?

What country has 63% of all hate crimes committed against Hispanics?

What country has people who do not take some 438,000,000 hours of earned vacation yearly?

What country is the only industrialized nation in the world that does not have government mandated time off from work for its people?

What country has people who have $7,800,000,000 worth of retail store gift cards that went unused in 2008?

What country has $704,000,000 worth of outstanding reward offers for terrorists, in 2008?

What country had an average of seventeen trucks daily crossing their southern border at Presidio in 2006, and is projected to have up to 800 per day when the NAFTA trade route highway gets built?

What country set the bail at $100,000 for a female southern lawyer who was accused of assault for vigorously shaking the hand of a fellow attorney?

What country has the average teacher's salary in one state at almost $60,000 per year, while in another state, the average is $34,000?

What country had some 250,000 soldiers and former soldiers suffering from the Iraq war's "signature wound," traumatic brain injury, in 2008?

What country's two most famous Hollywood war heroes (John Wayne and Sylvester Stallone) never served in the military?

What country will need to recruit 2,800,000 additional new teachers between 2008 and 2016, owing to baby boomer retirements, growing student enrollments, and staff turnover?

What country has some 72,000,000 dogs that produce about 274 pounds of poop each year, per pooch?

What country spent over $1,200,000,000,000 on Social Security, Medicare and Medicaid in 2007?

What country passed a law in 1996 that provided immunity to internet sites, so the hosts are not responsible for what users post there?

What country has estimated that 1,600,000 internet blog posts are created daily?

What country in 2008 had just one soldier from WWI still alive?

What country has had a 60% drop in duck hunting between 1953 and 2007?

What country has 90% of its two-year-olds who watch TV, DVDs or videos on a regular basis?

What country had the Standard and Poor's 500 stock index yield a limp 1.66% per year between 2000 and 2007?

What country gets 80% of the active ingredients in their medicines from sources outside of the country?

What country has learned that there were 3,000 satellites, launched by some forty different countries, circling the earth in 2008?

What country has 900,000 people who suffer heart attacks yearly, but just one in four recognize the symptoms?

What country has discovered that just 90,000 salmon returned to the Sacramento River in 2007, down from 800,000 in 2002?

What country no longer allows servicemen and women deployed to Iraq and Afghanistan to have beer?

What country had 50% of its West Point graduating class of 2001 opt out of the army by 2007?

What country has a $6,000,000,000 rebate industry where complaints have increased some 350% between 2002 and 2007?

What country had home values increase by 85% between 1997 and 2006?

What country has an unsold backlog of 1,000,000 single family homes and condominiums for sale in early 2008?

What country had 35,000 lobbyists in Washington, D.C., in 2008?

What country charges a $675 fee for an application for citizenship?

What country had an employee of a large health insurance company get $20,000 in bonuses over a six-year-period, essentially for canceling policies of risky clients?

What country had a judge award a victim of an insurance company's cancellation of her policy, after she was diagnosed with cancer . . . $9,000,000?

What country in 2008 had giant retail stores such as Wal-Mart, CVS, and Walgreens beginning to add shelf space for the sale of risqué products, including massage oils, lubricants, and vibrators?

What country has had online retail sales grow at a rate of 20% per year between 2003 and 2007?

What country is outraged by a proposed $233,000,000 "bridge to nowhere" in Alaska, but finds that that amount of money is spent in just eighteen hours in Iraq?

What country has a former governor in prison who has fifty-two former state attorneys general who have called for a review of his trial and conviction for accepting bribes?

What country had companies that in 2008 rented 12,000,000 bees for six weeks to farmers, for $27,000?

What country has found that honey bees are crucial to about one-third of all the foods that are eaten?

What country has learned that almost one-half of its people have left the religion of their childhood?

What country has 7,000,000 people who are completely illiterate, and another 27,000,000 who are unable to fill out a job application?

What country has a wood and paper industry that plants 1,700,000 new trees every day?

What country's press is the only industry protected by its Constitution?

What country has had 1,645 food recalls between 2001 and 2008?

What country provided trailers for the victims of a huge hurricane, only to discover that they had about five times the acceptable level of formaldehyde gas?

What country had blacks, Hispanics and Asians comprising 10% of its electorate in 1972, a figure that more than doubled by 2006?

What country has a system that freezes scrap tires and then pulverizes them so the powder can be used in products like paints, coatings, and sealants?

What country had nearly 40% of the credit card industry's $40,000,000,000 profit come from fees charged, in 2007?

What country learned that the average credit card debt soared from about $3,000 per household in 1990 to over $9,000 in 2008?

What country has learned that first-year college students participate in far less exercise than they did just one year before?

What country has women holding just 15% of board positions, despite the fact that they hold more than half of the management and professional jobs?

What country's dollar has been dropping in relation to other foreign currencies, for over five years?

What country in 2008 had one in every ninety-nine whites in prison, one in every thirty-six Hispanics in prison, and one in every fifteen blacks in its prisons?

What country had a major city report that 71% of teen pregnancies in its inner city resulted from statutory rape?

What country has nearly 7,000,000 of its kids under eighteen suffering from asthma?

What country had an authority on terrorism who pointed out that most terrorist attacks take place in democracies, not authoritarian countries?

What country introduced opium and cocaine in the 1800s as a cure for alcoholism?

What country has some 22,000,000 people who are hooked on the five-most difficult drugs to give up?

What country's federal budget for stopping drug flow and enforcement in 2008 is $8,300,000,000, but just $4,600,000,000 for treatment and prevention?

What country has estimated that if current trends continue, by 2030 some 8,000,000 people worldwide will die from tobacco-related illnesses each year?

What country has a sitting Supreme Court justice in 2008 who has never asked a question during the court's oral arguments for the past two years?

What country's gamblers learned that a British man had bet the equivalent of 98¢ on a combination of 8 horses, and won $1,900,000?

What country has witnessed an increase in people buying tiny offshore islands to the tune of from $200,000 to over $5,000,000 over the past ten years?

What country had over 177,000 people in 2007 who had weight-reduction surgeries?

What country has discovered that over 100,000 people are bitten by poisonous snakes every year, worldwide?

What country has 1,650 army recruiting offices?

What country had a major league baseball player who commanded a salary in 2007 that amounted to over $1,600,000 for every home run he hit?

What country has one in every 23 prison inmates who is fifty-five or older?

What country has some 4,000,000 people on Social Security or Supplementary Social Security who did not have bank accounts?

What country reviewed six states that implemented measures to insure that illegal immigrants were not getting Medicaid benefits, and found that for every $100 they spent implementing the rule, just 14¢ was saved?

What country has a pharmaceutical industry that spends just about 10% of the price of most brand-name pills to cover the cost of the raw materials and manufacturing?

What country had their pharmaceutical industry turn nearly 16¢ of every dollar of revenue into profit, in 2004, and was the nation's most profitable industry from 1995 to 2002?

What country tried a woman for murder after she admitted striking another woman over forty times with a heavy ax, and survived with just a few scratches, only to have the jury return a verdict of ''not guilty'' by reason of self-defense, after just two hours of deliberation?

What country in 2008, was paying tens of thousands of young Iraqi men $10 a day so they will not go back to being Iraqi insurgents?

What country has about one-third of their older folks who suffer a fall each year and about one-fourth of them lose some independence due to injury?

What country has up to 40% of nursing home admissions result from an inability to take medicines at home unsupervised?

What country has over 10,000 deaths due to SUV roll-overs each year?

What country loses over 1,500 people per day, to cancer?

What country has found that if you live in eastern states, it's actually ''greener'' to drink wine from France, than wine from a western state, due to the difference between emissions from trucks versus boats?

What country might have the chance in 2008 to join countries where over fifty women have been elected as heads of state, or prime ministers?

What country went from a prison population in 1987 of 585,000 to a population of 1,596,000 in 2007?

What country had one in every nine black men between the ages of twenty and thirty-four in prison, in 2008?

What country experienced 1,269 suicide deaths by people jumping off the Golden Gate Bridge, since 1937?

What country has about 600,000 hysterectomies performed yearly, and nearly 70% of them may be unnecessary?

What country has experienced skyrocketing drug arrests over the past three decades, while the arrest rate for murders has gone from nearly 90%, to less than half of that?

What country has a large western state where 80% of all prison inmates eventually leave prison, and 70% of those, come back?

What country's military is the largest consumer of oil in the world?

What country has learned that pigeons successfully delivered 95% of the messages given to them during combat in previous wars?

What country had a survey in 2000 that revealed that people are no happier than they were back in 1948 when wages were about two-thirds less?

What country's people took about 500,000 cruises in 1948, and over 6,500,000 in the year 2000?

What country had one car for every two people in 1948, and one car for every person of driving age, in 2000?

What country introduced sixty-six wolves into a national park in the 1990s and witnessed them growing to a population of over 1,500 in 2008?

What country has their large dogs putting some 300,000 people into their emergency hospital wards yearly?

What country had a President who was awarded the Nobel Peace Prize for mediating the Russo-Japanese War?

What country is devoting about one-third of its corn crop to make ethanol in 2008, more than triple the 2003 total?

What country has over 250,000,000 guns in the hands of its population?

What country had leases making up 27% of its new car sales in 2007?

What country will have over 50% of its teens trying illicit substances at least once, and almost all trying alcohol and tobacco, in any given year?

What country had over 670,000 people write to the government in an effort to get the polar bear on to the endangered species list?

What country has some 55,000 black churches?

What country replaced some 18,000 HumVees used in Iraq that cost $150,000 each, with upgraded mine-resistant vehicles that cost $800,000 each?

What country figured it cost about $180,000 per year for a sergeant in the Army, and $445,000 for a private security contractor, and spent over $4,000,000,000 on private security protection in 2007?

What country had 7,882 breast augmentation surgeries performed on teen girls in 2007?

What country has estimated that the world population will go from 6.6 billion in 2008, to 9.2 billion in 2050?

What country opened its first Piggly Wiggly grocery store in 1916, revolutionizing the retail market?

What country's people were saving about 10% of their disposable income in 1980, and just four-tenths of a percent in 2007?

What country's people are pretty much oblivious to a decade-old war in the Congo that has taken the lives of some 5,000,000 since 1998?

What country has over 1,000,000 high school athletes who have used illegal steroids?

What country has the average person buying a jet aircraft has a net worth of over $15,000,000, and the cost per airplane can go as high as $40,000,000?

What country has just 1% of their 28,000 daily commercial flights, with armed air marshals on board in 2008?

What country has an airline that paid $209,000,000 in 2008 for four sets of takeoff and landing slots at London's Heathrow airport?

What country in 1986 had a President who granted roughly 3,000,000 Hispanics amnesty, who were in the country illegally?

What country has nearly 150,000 people who are diagnosed with colorectal cancer yearly, with some 50,000 who die from it?

What country has learned that patients in Israel and Europe are using a tiny pill-shaped camera in 2008 that takes photos as it travels through the digestive system and transmits them to a data recorder worn on the patient's wrist?

What country saw an increase in 2005 of the top 1% of household incomes of $180,000, while middle-income households increased by $400 and lower-income households by just $200?

What country was expected to have over 28,000,000 people on food stamps in 2008?

What country's McDonald's fast food restaurants get about two-thirds of their income from drive-throughs?

What country has seen tea sales quadruple over the past decade and are expected to go from $6,000,000,000 to $10,000,000,000 by 2010?

What country is experiencing over 1,200,000 high school dropouts per year?

What country's truckers are made up of 90% independents?

What country's oil companies had $123,000,000,000 in profits in 2007?

What country has one large major city where just one out of every four high school students, graduates?

What country is ranked twenty-fourth in a report that measures countries by stability and prosperity . . . right behind Malta?

What country has had a Secretary of Defense who had five deferments from the draft, and never spent any time in the military?

What country's suspected terrorist "no-fly" list has ballooned to over 900,000 people in 2008?

What country has a former president who is partly responsible for the drop in the dreaded disease guinea worm from 3,500,000 in 1986 to about 10,000 in 2008 in African and Asian countries?

What country has had five Presidents who were cheerleaders during their school years?

What country has some 12,000,000 people who regularly lace up their running shoes and run, and 37,000,000 who do at least once a year?

What country has 50% of its population who are vitamin-D deficient, including 70% of the elderly and 90% of minorities, according to experts?

What country had a population of 128,000,000 and an unemployment rate of 22% in 1934?

What country has 35% of all of its families owning three or more cars?

What country has China holding over $500,000,000,000 of its treasury bonds?

What country during the 1960s spent 4% of its entire budget on NASA, but by 2007 that percentage was reduced to one-sixth of one per cent?

What country's average person's "bill" for NASA amounts to just 15¢ per day?

What country has had nearly 14,000 cases of molestation filed against the Catholic Church since 1950?

What country had nearly 350,000 women who had breast augmentation surgery in 2007, an increase of over 60% from the year 2000?

What country had about one-half of all of its adults who were smokers in the 1950s and just about one-fifth who were still smoking in 2008?

What country's life expectancy for a twenty-five-year-old man in 1990 with a high school education or less was about fifty years, while it was about seventy-five if he had attended college?

What country is experiencing Tylenol advertising in 2008 that there are ways to prevent common aches and pains without the help of Tylenol or any other pill?

What country has about 70% of its women who have kids younger than eighteen who work outside the home?

What country's average household spent nearly half of its $6,500 annual food budget out, in 2008?

What country consumes about sixty-six pounds of beef per person, fifty-one pounds of pork and less than one pound of lamb?

What country's military was against a bill in 2008 that would provide for free college education for veterans, with the reasoning that it would hurt their retention statistics?

What country has found that the unemployment rate among young veterans in 2008 was three times that of the national average?

What country's high schools have been underestimating their dropout rates by not counting those who promised to take their GED tests, and those who dropped out prior to the twelfth grade?

What country had 304,000 immigrants in their jails in 2008 who are eligible for deportation?

What country has about 58% of their college kids taking undergraduate courses, who are female?

What country has 29% of their people on Medicare who say they have trouble finding a doctor who would accept their insurance in 2007?

What country has 66% who say they had trouble getting medical care on nights, weekends, and holidays in 2007?

What country had just 30% who say they can get in to see their doctor on the same day, putting the country second to last among industrialized countries?

What country has one large state that had all of their 749 private practice physicians who would not accept new Medicare patients in 2007?

What country has the pay scale for a starting internist or family-practice physician at up to $150,000 per year, while specialists average about twice as much?

What country has a typical medical student graduating from college with a debt of $130,000?

What country has doctors who drop their longtime patients when they turn sixty-five, so they will not have to accept Medicare price guidelines?

What country's caesarean births went from 5% in 1970 to over 31% in 2007?

What country's doctors paid about $100,000 a year for malpractice insurance in 2007?

What country had almost 9,000 people in a survey of 26,000 who said his or her family had skipped medical care because of the cost?

What country had a minimum wage far below Great Britain's $10.71 in 2008?

What country is still putting 70,000 barrels of oil per day into their reserves, despite the fact that the price was hovering around $100 per barrel in 2008?

What country spends over $400,000,000,000 on foreign oil yearly?

What country has just about 2% of their high schools who have daily gym classes and less than 4% for elementary schools?

What country had half of the companies surveyed that offered employees financial rewards to persuade them to improve their health?

What country employed a new medical surgery technique where the patient's appendix was removed through his mouth?

What country in 2008 had over 516 golf courses that are certified "green" by an international Audubon organization?

What country has a new hybrid-electric car that gets 300 miles per gallon and sells for about $30,000 for a two-seater?

What country ranks 66th in a rating of countries for their environmental performance, behind countries like Iran, South Korea, Cuba, Malaysia, Latvia, and Mexico, among others?

What country witnessed the displacing of over 33,000,000 refugees, worldwide, in 2008?

What country had nearly 70% of the population who owned their own homes in 2004?

What country had a survey that determined that the average potential college student in 2008 was spending some $3,500 for just the process of applying to colleges?

What country has over 76,000,000 people who get food poisoning, yearly?

What country had a tax code with 67,506 pages of regulations and rulings in 2008?

What country has an inheritance tax that will take effect at midnight on December 31, 2010 that will have any inheritance over $1,000,000 subject to 55% tax?

What country has about 600,000,000 obsolete cell phones languishing in homes?

What country had the cost of government benefits to each person age sixty-five and over at $27,289 in 2008?

What country has about 218,000,000 people connected to the internet?

What country performs some 200,00 surgeries yearly using cadaver bones?

What country has over 97,000 people waiting for organ transplants in 2008, while China has over 2,000,000?

What country's average person will consume over 43,000 cans of soda in their lifetime?

What country in the 1960s banned interracial marriage in about half of the states?

What country in 2008 had women making up about one-third of the 24,000,000 golfers?

What country had their top three hedge fund managers who made $3,700,000,000, and $2,900,000,000 and $2,800,000,000 in 2007, and to make it into the top 50, the manager had to make over $250,000,000?

What country has a four-year waiting list for yachts that are priced at $15,000,000?

What country had a survey taken of 109 professional historians and found that 98 percent of them in 2008 believed that the Presidency has been a failure, and 61% say that the current presidency is the worst in the country's history?

What country went from having 2,620 pages of government regulations to 74,402 in 2008?

What country has five states that permit capital punishment for the rape of young children?

What country paid $300,000 a year for each anthropologist hired to try to find ways to gain local support in Iraqi villages . . . about six times the salary of others in their field?

What country's people spent $1,050,000,000 on Botox treatments for some 2,775,000 in 2007?

What country has about 1,000,000 children every year who watch their parents split up . . . triple the number of the 50s?

What country lost sixty kids in 2007 from being run over by vehicles in their own driveways?

What country, from 1995 to 2005, had over 50,000 people who had to be rescued off its West Coast, due to rip currents?

What country witnessed the news of an undersea earthquake in 2004 that was 23,000 times more powerful than the first atom bomb, and led to a huge tsunami?

What country has a Grand Canyon that is 227 miles long, one mile deep and eighteen miles across at its widest point?

What country has the results of an UN study that estimates there are 46,000 pieces of plastic floating per square mile of ocean?

What country produced 113,000,000,000 pounds of plastic in 2005?

What country's working class white adults went from 86% of its population in 1940 to just 48% on 2007?

What country has one large airline that has 655 planes and generated some $23,000,000,000 in sales in 2007?

What country generates almost one-fourth of the world's greenhouse gases each year?

What country has one large western state has the lowest per capita energy use of all 50 states, and its "green" policies have eliminated the need for twenty-four plants over the past thirty years?

242

What country has its doctors with the highest suicide rate of any profession with from 300 to 400 per year taking their own lives?

What country has 34,500,000 acres enrolled in the government program that paid farmers not to plant anything on that land, in 2008?

What country is second in the world when it comes to the amount of energy consumed per person per year, with over 340,000,000 btus per person, as opposed to a country like China with just 51,000,000 per person?

What country had some 186,000 prostate cancers diagnosed per year, but just five $100,000,000+proton beam facilities that can treat it very successfully, in 2008?

What country has about 15,000,000 people who have social phobia?

What country has a tree that can weigh up to 3,000,000 pounds?

What country experienced a rock slide in 1996 where a huge piece of granite, weighing some 90,000 tons, broke off and slammed down a hillside crushing everything in its path?

What country has had over 12,400,000 people who have undergone lasik eye surgery since the 1990s and growing at a rate of 700,000 per year?

What country has over 6,000,000 people who suffer from chronic dizziness or imbalance?

What country permits its Supreme Court justices to retire at their full salary?

What country has an estimated one in every five adults with genital herpes?

What country has estimated that 70% of their men over seventy have some form of prostate cancer?

What country's average wedding cost was $18,000 in 2008?

What country has ice sculptures for weddings that can run from $300 each to $50,000?

What country had 216,000,000 internet users in 2007, and was surpassed by China's 220,000,000 in 2008?

What country provides its farmers with a 51¢ subsidy per gallon of ethanol that is diverted from corn and feed grain supply?

What country has about 70% of high school girl freshmen sign up for physical education, but just some 32% are still taking it as seniors?

What country has one western city where seventeen different men have spent significant time in prison, (one for 27 years) only to be exonerated and freed, between 2001 and 2008?

What country has over 6,000,000 people who use cocaine regularly?

What country had a catastrophic failure of a top secret spy satellite launch that spewed some 4,000,000 pounds of rocket fuel and molten metal back on the earth?

What country has five times the number of truck drivers who are killed on the job, as policemen?

What country sends out some 19,000,000,000 catalogs every year, at a cost of 53,000,000 trees?

What country has a National Association of Unclaimed Property Administration that is holding over $32,000,000,000 worth of unclaimed bank accounts and other assets?

What country has estimated that 1,000,000 new babies are born into this world every 4 days?

What country has witnessed seventy-nine journalist murders in Iraq without any of them being solved, since the inception of the Iraqi war?

What country has witnessed an uptick in the consumption of raw unpasturized milk, despite the fact that there were forty-five outbreaks of disease that were traced to the practice, between 1998 and 2005?

What country has recently found that Macao, China, has overtaken Las Vegas, Nevada, in gambling revenue?

What country has been witness to the building of a huge gambling casino in Macao, China that has 16,000 employees and had over 10,000,000 visitors during their first six months of operation?

What country had 15,500,000 people who are behind on their utility payments in 2008?

What country passed a law that allows the postal service to raise its prices every May?

What country had the Mount Rushmore sculpture of four presidents made for just $1,000,000?

What country has an internet dating service that claims to have over 230 of their users who marry every day?

What country had Nelson Mandela, South Africa's Nobel Peace Prize winner, on its terrorist watch list?

What country had a magician who held his breath for a record seventeen minutes and four seconds?

What country has seen its "Mall of America" go from the largest shopping mall in the world, to one that won't even make the top ten in 2008?

What country, despite the fears, has discovered that its citizens have more of a chance of drowning in their own bathtub than they have being killed in a terrorist attack?

What country pretty much credits itself with defeating the Germans during WWII, while a full 75% of German forces were engaged against the Russians on the Eastern front during the waning years of the war?

What country graduated some 75,000 engineers in 2004 while China was graduating 950,000?

What country has projected that 75% of all science Ph.D. degrees in 2010 will be awarded to its foreign students?

What country is one of just three countries in the world that does not use the metric system, along with Liberia and Myanmar?

What country has over 25,000,000 people who work just part-time?

What country secretly bargained away its missiles in Turkey during the so-called "Cuban Missile Crisis," and did not make that fact public for decades?

What country graduates less than half of its black students within six years of entering four-year college institutions, while Yale University graduates over 96% of its students?

What country in 2008 had a President who was against the passage of a bill that passed by a vote of ninety-seven to one in the Senate?

What country catches about 30,000,000 of the 40,000,000 salmon that return to their rivers to breed, every year?

What country dropped out of international competition that compared math students, in 2008?

What country had one Girl Scout who sold a record of over 17,000 boxes of Girl Scout cookies?

What country makes movies that receive over 50% of their box office revenues from foreign market places?

What country has over 9% of those 47,000,000 who did not have health insurance making over $75,000 per year?

What country has an average of over two cars per household, while China has just one car for every seventy households in 2008?

What country has seventy-seven lobbyists for every member of Congress in Washington, D.C.?

What country has 70% of their eighth graders who are not proficient in reading?

What country had over 13,000 Japanese-Americans who ultimately served in WWII and suffered over 9,000 casualties?

What country provides some $2,000,000,000 in foreign-bound food aid annually, from surplus crops purchased by the government?

What country had a drug raid on a prestigious fraternity at a popular state university that yielded four pounds of cocaine,

350 Ecstasy pills, fifty pounds of marijuana, thirty vials of hash oil and $60,000 in cash?

What country has "the world's largest adult sex and swingers web site" that has over 18,000,000 members?

What country has weight-loss camps that charge adults $6,500 and kids $2,500 for two weeks?

What country makes up about 5% of the world's population of 6.6 billion?

What country in 2008 had just 1% of its population that considers crime as their top issue?

What country had 72% of all income gains from 2002 to 2006 that went to the top 1% . . . households making more than $382,000 per year?

What country found in 2005 that about half of all personal bankruptcies were at least partly attributable to medical costs?

What country has even its homeless people with carbon footprints of 8.5 tons per year . . . twice the global average?

What country saw the veterans' requests for homelessness assistance increase by 600% between 2007 and 2008?

What country has 75% of the households where children are being home-schooled are Evangelical Christians?

What country has a large airline that claims it costs them an additional $800,000,000 for every rise of $10 in the price of a barrel of oil?

What country has over half of their college graduates moving back home to live with their parents?

What country had over 500,000 children in foster homes in 2008?

What country has the highest teen-age pregnancy rate in the Western world?

What country discovered that a British coin dealer had what was thought to be the only surviving 1933 Gold Double eagle coin from a government meltdown, and split the $7,590,000 it was sold for at auction, with the dealer?

What country experienced a rash of thefts of thousands of manhole covers in 2008 due to the spike in scrap metal prices?

What country had over 75,000 people waiting for kidney transplants in 2008 and some 10,000 of them will receive transplants from deceased strangers?

What country has 53% of the population that consider themselves "middle class," 19% who consider themselves "upper middle class," 19% who consider themselves "lower middle class," 2% who consider themselves "upper class," and 6% who consider themselves, "lower class"?

What country had a billionaire computer genius and his wife contribute $1,800,000,000 to the country's public high schools?

What country had a President who, on his last day in office, pardoned a man whose wife had contributed nearly $500,000 to his presidential library?

What country has nearly 1,000,000 people who are severely paralyzed?

What country finds one of its largest cities ranking fifteenth on the list of most expensive cities to live in, while Moscow is number one and London is number 2?

What country had one large city that was required to pay over $155,000,000 to settle claims of police misconduct and brutality over a five-year period?

What country had a long-playing Lawrence Welk musical show on TV where tickets were sold out for eighteen months in advance, most of the time?

What country has about two-thirds, or $260,000,000,000 of its currency, being held in foreign countries in 2008?

What country in 1999 arrested nearly 4,000 counterfeiters?

What country had a bidding war between two popular magazines for the first rights to public photos of twins expected by a Hollywood couple, that reached over $15,000,000 in 2008?

What country had an increase in the S & P 500 of 10.7% annually between 1945 and 2007 when Democrats occupied the

White House, and just 7.6% during the same period when Republicans occupied the White House?

What country loses over 500,000 people annually, to cancer?

What country has an estimated 5,000 babies born yearly through sperm donations, and another 10,000 from donor eggs?

What country has put over 2,500 juveniles in prison in Iraq, Afghanistan and Guantanamo, the youngest being ten years old?

What country must spend $228,000,000 to replace money printing plates and presses to comply with a court ruling that their paper money discriminates against the blind?

What country has some 9,000 people yearly who are told they have a fast-growing malignant brain cancer?

What country lost nearly 100 men during the construction of a huge western dam?

What country has a 1994 law that prohibits taking race into consideration when making adoptions?

What country had $1,600,000,000,000 in exports in 2007, a record high?

What country has almost 40% of its women who haven't worn a pair of nylons in a year?

What country has about half of its work force who have worn blue jeans to work recently, in 2008?

What country's army flew unmanned drones in Iraq and Afghanistan for over 46,000 hours in just one month in 2008?

What country had an unmanned drone program where the drones crashed after every twenty flight hours or so, cost $3,000,000 per copy, and was finally cancelled after burning up about $1,000,000,000 of taxpayers' money?

What country has developed unmanned drone aircraft that are capable of carrying four Hellfire missiles and two 500-pound bombs?

What country has roughly 1,500 drones flying in Iraq and Afghanistan, in 2008?

What country had the CEO of Wal-Mart usually come out in favor of raising the minimum wage law?

What country had a study that revealed in 2005 that teens who took a pledge of abstinence were six times as likely to have engaged in oral sex as teen virgins who hadn't taken the pledge?

What country prosecuted a female twenty-seven-year old teacher for having sex with a boy student and faced up to 100 years in prison?

What country has over $100,000,000,000 in gift card sales, and some 27% of the recipients never use them, leaving $8,000,000,000 unspent?

What country has over 90,000 women per year who report being raped?

What country's highly acclaimed Yale University first admitted women in the year 1968?

What country made the birth control pill legal in 1965?

What country dropped 5,019 bombs in the occupied countries of Iraq and Afghanistan in 2007 . . . up from 371 in 2004?

What country allows couples to exclude up to $500,000 in capital gains from the sale of a private residence?

What country has about 43% of its companies that monitor their employees' use of e-mail?

What country's public medical school graduates average about $120,000 in debt, while private school graduates average $160,000?

What country has nearly one-third of adults who take five or more medicines or suppliments every day?

What country has about 18,000,000 people who visit hospital emergency rooms yearly because they've taken medications incorrectly?

What country's people spent $287,000,000,000 on prescription drugs in 2007 . . . just five times as much as in 1993?

What country had a multi-term President who once claimed to have written the Constitution of Haiti, and was proven to be a false claim?

What country has life insurance companies that made 67¢ profit for every $1.00 that they take in on premiums?

What country had 2,500,000 college graduates in the year 2008?

What country has a population where just 10% hold passports?

What country has one state where average Medicare spending for the last two years of a patient's life is $181,143 and another state where it's just $29,116?

What country in 2008 had Medicare that will soon stop paying for most treatment of bedsores and hospital infections in an effort to discontinue the practice of hospitals actually making money from treating their own mistakes?

What country has the top 300,000 who have more income than the bottom 200,000,000?

What country had a President who lied about having a U-2 spy plane flying over the USSR until they made public that they had shot it down and had the pilot in custody?

What country does not allow its soldiers in Afghanistan to have a beer, despite the fact that their allies permit their soldiers over there to have it?

What country buys oil from a country that boasts about serving a cocktail drink to patrons that costs $7,440 a pop?

What country witnessed the explosion of Gulf economies between 2002 and 2006 where their economies actually doubled?

What country has over 1,000,000 vehicles stolen, yearly?

What country has car theft as a yearly $8,500,000,000 problem?

What country had the median price for a single family home at $48,000 in 1977 and $247,000 in 2007?

What country cannot sell its cars in China because they don't meet the Chinese environmental standards?

What country leased 68,000,000 acres of federal land to the oil and gas industry, that was not being utilized in 2008, one half off-shore and about one-half inland?

What country in 2008 had some 20,000 disabled soldiers who have been discharged over the past few years facing a military bureaucracy that makes soldiers wait for six to nine months before their full disability payments begin?

What country has estimated that about two-thirds of all vehicle accidents are the result of aggressive driving?

What country had a major league baseball player set a record of eleven straight hits being home runs?

What country has a major city where over 1,000 youths are regularly arrested for carrying a gun, and one-third were seventeen years old and younger?

What country had over 350,000 acres of land in 2007 devoted to growing tobacco, despite the fact that an estimated 5,000,000 people in the world die of tobacco related illnesses?

What country had about 45,000,000 of its people who still smoked in 2007?

What country in 2008 had a high school of just over 1,000 students where seventeen girls joined a "pact" to get pregnant, and did, at age sixteen and younger?

What country had a woman who left $12,000,000 to her pet dog, at her death, and later a judge reduced it to $2,000,000 when it was learned that the dog's expenses were just $190,000 per year?

What country in 2008 had over 1,000,000 gas/electric hybrid cars on the road?

What country had a high school where a school nurse reported to have administered over 150 pregnancy tests to women students?

What country has estimated that over 300,000 retail workers are victims of workplace violence, yearly?

What country had 260 kids killed in schools during a nine year period?

What country has a video game called "Grand Theft Auto" that brought in over $500,000,000 during its first week of sales?

What country supplies amphetamines to its fighter pilots?

What country had no bank failures between 2004 and 2007 where the Federal Deposit Insurance had to come to the rescue, but there were four during the first few months of 2008?

What country had a sitting President in 1992 who garnered just 37% of the election popular vote, and lost re-election?

What country had home owners who used the equity in their homes as ATMs in 2006 by taking out $350,000,000,000 in home-equity loans or second mortgages?

What country had an average gain of 150,000 new jobs per month over the fifteen years preceding 2008?

What country's government spent over $8,000,000,000 on salmon recovery projects and yet the fish were declining at a rapid rate in 2008?

What country has spent almost $500,000,000 on TV broadcasting news and propaganda to Arabs over four years, and yet a survey revealed that just 2% watch it?

What country witnessed WWI military veterans march on the capital in an effort to obtain benefits, only to be greeted with gunfire that killed some and wounded many?

What country had a President who said he was willing to go to the brink to stop Red China from bombarding Quemoy and Matsu, two tiny islands off the coast of China in the Strait of Formosa. (Taiwan)

What country has discovered that Doctors Without Borders has developed a peanut-butter-like concoction called Plumpy nuts that could go a long way toward solving the problem of 5,000,000 children world-wide dying from malnutrition every year?

What country has 49% of its population that believes that the President can suspend the Constitution?

What country has witnessed China requiring all of their citizens over forty to have their waist measured and if a man has a waist over 33½", he must undergo counseling and requires close monitoring?

What country has over 8% of their families who have a net worth of over $1,000,000?

What country in 2007 had elective eyelid surgery as the second most popular cosmetic procedure for men?

What country uses almost one-fourth of all of the world's daily consumption of oil and gas?

What country has 475,000 school busses that carry some 25,000,000 kids?

What country could reduce all cancers by 70% if they exercised regularly, ate less red meat, grew thinner, ate diets rich in fruits and vegetables, and stopped using tobacco?

What country has prostate, colon and breast cancers that are extremely common, while other countries have these cancers just one-twentieth the rate?

What country in 2008 was averaging $28,000 for weddings, with some including tower cakes that cost $5,000?

What country had estimated that some 750,000 teens will get pregnant in 2008?

What country spent about $1,500,000,000 on government-sponsored "abstinence only" programming for youngsters between 2001 and 2008?

What country has 81,000,000 people who either have diabetes or have a pre-diabetic condition?

What country's average person stands in line for two years of his/her life?

What country had five states that permit the death penalty in cases of child rape but it was overturned by the Supreme Court in 2008 citing the fact that over 5,000 cases of child rape are reported yearly?

What country had 9,800 people end up in hospital emergency wards due to handling fireworks in 2007?

What country generated over 1,500,000 tons of electronic waste to landfills in 2007?

What country has a company that claims to have sold over 100,000,000 capsules that they say will "make a certain part of the male body larger?"

What country in 2008 has electronic gadgets that warn you audibly in your car, when you are approaching an intersection where cameras have been installed to catch red light violators?

What country has gas service station owners paying some $40,000 to fill up their undergorund gas tanks?

What country that pays $3.77 for a gallon of gasoline, sees it going 10¢ to the service station, 38¢ to the refiner, 38¢ for taxes, and $2.83 for the crude oil?

What country has 37% of its people who nap on a daily basis?

What country had a six-year study that revealed that people who nap at least three times a week have a reduced risk of death by heart attack by almost 40%?

What country's personal savings rate actually turned negative in 2005?

What country has an estimated 60% of the 100,000 people awaiting organ donations will die before getting them?

What country has more prescription drug abusers than those addicted to amphetamines, cocaine and heroin, combined?

What country stood by silently for twenty-seven years while South America imprisoned Nelson Mandela?

What country had a public school system in a large midwestern city, give a car to a twelve-year-old girl for her perfect school attendance?

What country has its largest auto company's stock worth about $6,500,000,000 in 2008 while Toyota's is worth $163,000,000,000?

What country had 6,000,000 of its people living abroad in 2008?

What country got most of its oil from Canada, followed by Saudi Arabia, Mexico, Venezuela and Nigeria, in 2008?

What country had fourteen Medivac helicopters crash in 2006?

What country has a southern state that purchased 187,000 acres from a large sugar producing company, for $1,750,000,000 in 2008?

What country's Transportation Security Administration collected about $1,000,000 between 2005 and 2008 from travelers who left loose change at their checkpoints?

What country used air conditioning energy in 2006 that was more than the total energy usage of about 140 other countries?

What country began a large dam project in Afghanistan back in the 1940s and was still attempting to finish it in 2008?

What country has a large hamburger fast food operation that was selling about 60% more chicken in 2008 than it did in 2003?

What country has seen housing prices in metropolitan areas rise six times as fast as household incomes between 1988 and 2008?

What country is impounding travelers' laptops at airports and keeping them for weeks and months while examining the contents, leaving open the question of other nations beginning to do the same to their citizens?

What country has found their teen summer employment rate in 2008 to be the worst jobless rate in sixty-one years?

What country had a woman CEO who oversaw the expansion of an internet company go from $47,000,000 to $7,600,000,000 during her tenure?

What country in 2008 was behind Brazil in exports of beef, poultry, soybeans, sugar, coffee and orange juice?

What country processed thousands of chickens and pigs for market daily, but could not match 500,000 chickens and 5,000 pigs daily processed by Brazil in 2008?

What country was aided in its Revolution against Britain, by not only France, but by Spain and Holland as well?

What country launched just a handful of warships against the British in the Revolutionary War, but had more than 2,000 privateer ships that engaged the British navy and where some 12,000 were held in British prison ships and eventually thrown overboard to drown during the war?

What country's first President was given the name "Town Destroyer" by the Iroquois Indians after he authorized the "total destruction and devastation" of their settlements in upstate New York?

What country experienced the price of a typical $252,000 home in 2000 plunge to $150,000 in 2006?

What country had an estimated 1,000,000 kids with autism in 2008?

What country has to rescue by helicopter about 400 people per year who attempt to hike down the Grand Canyon, and are injured or overcome by the heat?

What country had an ultra-conservative radio talk show host who received a $40,000,000 contract in 2008?

What country has an estimated 31,000 grizzly bears in a northern state?

What country saw seventy weather-related events between 1980 and 2006 that resulted in over $1,000,000,000 in damage?

What country has one county in a large western state that has about 30,000 of its homeowners defaulting on their property taxes, yearly?

What country has 4,925 books in its Library of Congress written about its former president, Abraham Lincoln?

What country spent $5,000,000,000 in response to a total of five deaths from anthrax?

What country had a former general who became president and proceeded to turn down several requests for new weapons systems and missiles, and instead used defense dollars to build an interstate highway system?

What country had a President who prohibited scientists from using federal money for studies on any stem-cell lines except those seventy-one that were in existence in 2001 and by 2008, sixty-five of them having proved useless?

What country's men signed up for 21,311 breast reduction procedures for themselves in 2007?

What country in 2008 had the cost of public elementary or high school average annual cost at just over $400, while private day school median tuition is over $16,000?

What country had the average tuition, room and board cost of a public four-year college in 2008 at less than $14,000, while the same costs for a private four-year college average was over $32,000?

What country, along with Britain, during WWII was responsible for the carpet bombing of Dresden, Germany, and the loss of some 250,000 people in a twenty-four-hour period?

What company had made sixty-two Legos for every man, woman and child in the world, and continues to make about 19,000,000,000 yearly?

What country has 3,000 children who die annually on bicycles and some 29,000 who end up in hospitals?

What country has a company that can make 300,000 hot dogs in an hour?

What country has a federal criminal justice system that has no provision for parole of prison inmates?

What country has over one-third of their adolescents who fail to meet the current physical activity requirements?

What country has one city with over 13,000 taxi cabs?

What country has three states that flat-out ban the sale of tickets for more than their face value?

What country's families spent some 44% of their food budget in 2006, on eating out?

What country, over the past fifty years, has granted subsidies for the coal, oil, gas, and nuclear industries twelve times more than those for renewable energy sources such as wind, solar, and biofuels?

What country's CIA used LSD in experiments long before it was used as a recreational drug, by giving it to incarcerated prison inmates who were drug addicts, and promising them heroin in return for their participation?

What country had captured pilots who confessed to dropping biological weapons over North Korea during the Korean conflict?

What country that has always prided itself on its auto industry, is learned that China was putting some 25,000 new cars on their roads every day in 2008?

What country was making pennies in 2008 that cost them nearly 2¢ each, and nickels that cost about a dime?

What country had a high-ranking civilian Pentagon official describe the reason for the invasion of Iraq as "anticipatory self-defense?"

What country spends about 6¢ making each of its paper bills, from the $1 to the $5 and $10 and on up?

What country has a large eastern state where there is a criminal court that has been set up especially for veterans and tends to be more lenient and considers mental problems more than the average court?

What country's average worker travels twenty-eight miles, to and from work?

What country's FBI and ATF lost some credibility with their aggressive actions at Ruby Ridge and Waco?

What country has made it illegal to sell organs but permits trading organs?

What country's hospitals typically give insurance companies a discount of 60% on a hospital reimbursement?

What country's hospitals had some $31,200,000,000 in uncompensated care costs in 2006?

What country had a film documentary that claimed Wal-Mart costs taxpayers $1,557,000,000 to support their low-paid employees?

What country had its fourth largest city located in the midwest in 1900, that can't make the top 50 cities in 2008?

What country loses $9,000,000,000 in productivity a year from commercial flight delays alone?

What country's eBay was ordered to pay nearly $63,000,000 by a French court to a group of luxury brands for not doing enough to deter the sale of rip-offs?

What country has states that charge maybe $100 for vanity license plates, while Arab businessmen in Abu Dhabi actually spend millions to obtain single-digit plates?

What country has discovered that their people ages five through thirty-four are more likely to die in traffic accidents than any other way?

What country bought the state of Alaska in 1867 for $7,200,000 from Russia?

What country had Teddy Roosevelt, shortly after becoming president, declare that "In God We Trust" should be removed from its coins?

What country had one of its most popular humorists declare, "No nation, however mighty, occupies a foot of land that was not stolen?"

What country has the book "Huckleberry Finn" as one of the most books frequently kicked off of its library shelves?

What country has canine hip replacement surgery that costs $8,000?

What country in 1964 had 90% silver in its 50¢ pieces, reduced to 40% in 1965 and further reduced to 0 in 1971?

What country has 285,000 hip-replacement surgeries performed yearly?

What country spends about $500,000,000,000 on unnecessary care?

What country has 70% of black families headed by just one person?

What country's funerals use 30,000,000 board feet of casket wood, 90,000 tons of steel, 1,600,000 tons of concrete and 800,000 gallons of embalming fluid?

What country has the highest percentage of people who own their own homes of any country in the world?

What country has a prison population that has gone up 1000% in thirty years?

What country has one company that has brought down over 7,000 structures with explosives, including bridges, large buildings, arenas, and towers?

What country had to use twenty-two tons of explosives to bring down an old stadium?

What country has some 80,000 prison inmates who are in solitary confinement at any one time?

What country has some 1,600 different, functioning gangs in its prisons?

What country has about one in five prison inmates who admit to having been sexually victimized, amounting to over some 400,000?

What country has just twelve out of 5,000 prisons who have a higher education program?

What country releases about 700,000 prison inmates into the public, every year?

What country passed a law that allows its law enforcement officials to go into other sovereign countries to kidnap their citizens?

What country puts people in jail for gambling, and at the same time allows nearly every state to have lotteries?

What country sends people to jail for life for growing a tall, green plant?

What country refused to sign an international agreement signed by nearly every other country in the world, to discontinue the use of land mines?

What country pays its CEOs of large corporations hundreds of millions of dollars per year, at the same time that their workers are paid just over $5 per hour?

What country would send people to prison for smoking a cigarette that makes them feel good?

What country requires a state license for a hair dresser, but none for a person to buy a pistol?

What country allows its border patrol officers to use deadly force in a situation where minor law-breakers wield rocks?

What country sends sometimes three police cars with sirens wailing, to a verbal domestic dispute?

What country continues to subsidize the tobacco industry?

What country dropped atomic bombs on two cities in Japan during WWII, with no pretense of them being military targets?

What country had a warship mistakenly shoot down a commercial airliner with a missile, killing 300 people, with no apology?

What country pays some star athletes over $20,000,000 per year, at the same time they pay their school teachers about $30,000 per year?

What country allowed some seventy law enforcement officers to attack a large home full of devout religious men, women and children, that ultimately resulted in the death by fire of twenty-seven children and forty adults?

What country allowed its soldiers to take live ammunition onto a college campus, and fired upon the students, resulting in some injuries and deaths, and none were ever punished?

What country had a battleship stand offshore and lob 2,000 pound shells into the city of Beirut, Lebanon?

What country launched an unprovoked missile attack on a suspected chemical plant in a foreign country, only to discover later that it was not a chemical plant?

What country has the popular saying that ''It is better to be guilty of a crime and rich, than innocent of a crime and poor''?

What country assembled a force of eighty law enforcement officers outside of a public school where shots were being fired inside, and yet not enter the building for four hours while people bled to death?

What country requires students to take geometry courses, but not courses on marriage?

What country has some 130,000 women who get breast implants yearly?

What country has an estimated 70,000,000 people who have used marijuana?

What country is ranked thirty-seventh among other nations in the category of overall fairness and quality of health care, right behind Cosa Rica?

What country has 23% of their children who are living below the poverty level, while a country like Sweden has just 2%?

What country devotes over $35,000,000,000 yearly to maintain its arsenal of nuclear weapons, that is equal to 100,000 Hiroshima-type bombs?

What country "liberated" Okinawa during WWII, and has refused to leave for the next 6 decades?

What country's police respond to over 200,000 calls from public school officials per year?

What country has some 240,000,000 guns in its civilians' hands, mostly handguns that are of little use for hunting?

What country has over 400 firms that are in the business of predicting how a potential juror will vote in a criminal trial, with a reported 96% success, who charge over $100,000 for their services?

What country has over 500,000 kids living with foster care parents?

What country has four times the murder rate per capita of Britain?

What country allowed a gangster into its "witness protection" program, knowing that he participated in the murder of nineteen people, because he agreed to testify against a higher-ranking gangster?

What country designated "drop-off" points for young mothers to take their newborn infants to, in an effort to stop the mothers from killing their babies?

What country has over 20,000 of its people who are murdered, yearly?

What country continues to spend hundreds of billions of dollars every year on military spending, while over 300,000 children are dying of starvation and preventable illnesses, every day around the world?

What country has three-fourths of all of the world's serial killers?

What country went to war against another country when their own political leaders voted just 51 to 48 in favor of it?

What country has about 4 percent of the world's population, but 25 percent of the world's prison population?

What country has over 300,000 mentally ill people in their prisons?

What country has 4,000 cars stolen every day, and arrests only about 15 percent of the thieves?

What country has found that twenty-five years ago, one woman committed violence to every ten men, but in 2008, the figure was 1 in 4?

What country has discovered that motorcycles are five times more deadly than autos?

What country finds that losing one pound takes four pounds of pressure off of your knees?

What country sold the last known 1903 Model A Ford for $693,000 at auction in 2008?

What country finds that 60 percent of their black high school dropouts will end up behind bars?

What country has approximately 25,000,000 lightning strikes per year, resulting in eighteen deaths during the first six months of 2008?

What country's scientists have determined that a person has 250,000 sweat glands in a human foot?

What country has a Post Office with 220,000 vehicles?

What country sold a baseball cap that had been worn by Babe Ruth, for $285,000 at auction?

What country had a survey in 2008 that revealed that 78 percent of its work force felt "burned out"?

What country has some huge cargo ships that can carry 11,000 mammoth shipping containers?

What country had an estimated 175,000 chronically homeless in 2005?

What country has Mormons making up almost one-half of the population of Las Vegas?

What country has some 20,000,000 huge ship containers in operation at any one time, on the sea and in its ports?

What country exports about 1,400,000 barrels of petroleum products every day?

What country had one state that spent $524,000,000 in 2007 fighting fires?

What country has plans to launch astronauts to the moon again, by 2020 and then to Mars by 2030 . . . a round trip that will take two and one-half years?

What country's Major League Baseball teams had revenues of $3,900,000,000 in 2003 and $6,100,000,000 in 2007?

What country has 39 percent of its adult parents who support adult children, and 8 percent who support their elderly parents?

What country has an FBI organization that went from thirty-four agents in 1908 to some 12,000 personnel in 2008?

What country's scientific community has revealed that there are over 3,500,000 so-called test tube babies that have been born since 1988 worldwide?

What country experiences some 30,000 nail gun injuries yearly, and some 800,000 power tool injuries?

What country produces over 250,000,000 tons of garbage, yearly?

What country developed the first cordless, battery-powered drill for use by astronauts who needed it to drill soil samples on the moon?

What country's coins last an average of thirty years, while their paper money lasts just about eighteen months?

What country had about 80,000 pay telephones in 1902, and over 2,600,000 in the 1990s?

What country puts 3,500,000 coins in vending machines every fifteen minutes of every day?

What country has over 7,000,000 people born to parents of different races?

What country has 50% of its 28,000,000 children ages eight to twelve who regularly use cell phones, and might be at risk?

What country has 42 percent of its people who have tried marijuana, the highest of any country surveyed?

What country's doctors write over 40,000,000 prescriptions for sleeping pills every year?

What country supports the government of Afghanistan even though its ranking in the corruption index of 179 countries, is 172?

What country cut a deal with a gangster who admitted to killing twenty people, and sent him to prison for fourteen years where he served twelve and was out on the street in 2008?

What country has 563,000 truck and bus drivers who have significant ailments and receive full federal disability payments?

What country has one out of every eight residents of the District of Columbia who is an attorney?

What country has a "Don't Ask, Don't Tell" policy for their gays in the military while Britain allows gays to openly live together in military housing?

What country's $1 bill is worth $100,000,000,000,000 of Zimbabwe's newest bank note, where inflation is raging at 2,200,000 percent?

What country has just one-half the suicide rate of Japan?

What country still has fifteen states that have laws on the books restricting Sunday sales of alcohol?

What country has thirteen states that recently repealed the laws restricting the sale of alcohol on Sundays, which led to a 15 percent drop in weekly church attendance and a 25 percent drop in donations?

What country's airline industry had a fuel bill of some $16,000,000,000 in 2000, and was expected to reach over $60,000,000,000 in 2008?

What country had some 27,000,000 tons of plastic that ended up in their landfills in 2005?

What country has over 3,600 high school gay-straight alliances that are designed to foster the acceptance of gay students?

What country has learned that the Japanese Emperor Hirohito, in his surrender broadcast to the people, after the atomic bombs struck Hiroshima and Nagasaki, said, ''The war situation has developed not necessarily to Japan's advantage''?

What country has found that one-third of female troops in the military have been sexually assaulted, and just 8 percent of those accused of rape are ever court-martialed?

What country was #1 in college-graduate rates in 1983 and by 2008 had slipped to #21?

What country's scientists have estimated that we have only identified about 10 percent of the world's insects?

What country's banking industry vigorously opposed the creation of the FDIC back in 1933, claiming that it was ''unsound, unscientific, unjust and dangerous''?

What country's FDIC has ninety banks on its ''problem'' list, and five had actually failed during the first six months of 2008?

What country has sold $5,700,000,000,000 in stocks and bonds to foreigners between 2001 and 2007?

What country has estimated that the world population of the middle class will increase by 2,000,000,000 by the year 2030, using people with incomes of from $6,000 to $30,000 to define "middle class"?

What country had the top Attorney General declare that an individual scientist was a "person of interest" in the investigation of the anthrax case, only to determine later that he was innocent, and the government had to pay him $5,800,000 for ruining his life?

What country's IRS has decreased their audits of the largest corporations by 50 percent from 1988 to 2008, while doubling the audits on individual tax payers between 2000 and 2008?

What country's best known auction company racked up $3,500,000,000 in art sales in the first half of 2008 during a sagging economy, up some 56 percent from 2006?

What country complains about their congressmen and women taking expensive trips abroad, while Britain spent $760,000 for chartering a flight for a visit from the Queen of England, and an additional $560,000 for a visit to the Caribbean by Prince Charles and his wife?

What country shows little interest in "roundabouts" made famous in Britain, despite the fact that one-half of all road crashes occur at their intersections?

What country has seen faith-based funds increase from $500,000,000 to nearly $17,000,000,000 from 1998 to 2008?

What country has normalized relations with Viet Nam and seen the growth of trade mushroom from $1,200,000,000 in 2001 to $12,000,000,000 in 2007?

What country was instrumental in changing the Olympic rules for basketball, to allow their professionals to play, only to be beaten by countries like Argentina, Greece, and Puerto Rico?

What country has 75 percent of its people in favor of gays being able to serve openly in the military?

What country had about 40,000 escalator-related injuries among adults age sixty-five and over between 1991 and 2005?

What country's teen boys have adopted a style of sagging pants, which in part was triggered by prison inmates who had sagging pants due to the fact that they weren't allowed to have belts?

What country had a survey that revealed that people who kept a ''food diary'' while on a diet, lost twice as much weight as those who did not?

What country had a federally subsidized rail company that has never shown a profit in its thirty-seven-year history?

What country inserts a small amount of metal into their ceramic knives, to insure that they cannot be carried onto commercial aircraft?

What country has 142,000 vehicles that run on natural gas?

What country has recognized a huge ''Great Pacific Garbage Patch'' about 1,000 miles off of its West coast where a swirling mass of plastic debris, twice the size of Texas, exists?

What country's largest auto manufacturer sold more Buicks to China in 2007, than in their own home country?

What country is widely known as the auto capital of the world, but has learned that China puts over 25,000 new cars on their roads every day?

What country has witnessed the price of cocaine drop 80 percent since 1981?

What country has just one eastern state where three times as many heroin addicts overdose as in all of the Netherlands, where it is not illegal?

What country has about 16 percent of its population who try cocaine in their lifetime whereas the rate in the Netherlands is less than 2 percent?

What country had a survey in 2008 that revealed some 1,600,000 households have determined to relocate abroad, and an additional 1,800,000 who were seriously considering it, and 7,700,000 more who were "somewhat seriously" considering it?

What country is the only developed nation that taxes the earnings of its people living abroad who are also paying foreign income taxes?

What country imported over $321,000,000,000 worth of goods from China in 2007?

What country has discovered that their cows are major contributors to global warming because they generate methane?

What country has just 3 percent of its people who are vegetarians whereas a country like India has about 33 percent?

What country consumes just about 2 percent of its energy from renewable sources in 2008?

What country's Academy of Pediatrics recently told its Pediatricians to prescribe statins to children as young as eight years old if they had a predisposition for high cholesterol and were overweight?

What country vigorously regulates the cosmetic industry, but does not regulate the tattoo industry?

What country has been warned by officials that over 72,000 of their bridges are "structurally deficient"?

What country granted former slaves the right to vote in the 15th Amendment of 1869, but only for male ex-slaves?

What country has over 56,000 new cases of HIV infection yearly?

What country had a Baseball Major League expansion in 1960 where the new team paid just a bit over $2,000,000 for its entire roster?

What country has experienced twenty-six railway derailments, some catastrophic, due to displaced bridges, since 1982?

What country had a person who paid $1,620,000 for an old baseball card?

What country pays less than every country in the developed world, except Korea and Mexico, in income taxes?

What country has witnessed its Olympic Basketball Team's margin of victory over the past four Olympics go from 43 to 32, to 21, and then to just 4?

What country discovered in 2008 that some 41,000,000 credit card numbers had been stolen between 2005 and 2007?

What country won eight Olympic medals for diving in 1984, then in subsequent Olympics, 5, 3, 2, 1, and finally none in 2004?

What country has been impressed by China's modern train that reaches speeds of almost 300 mph?

What country has just twenty-six characters in their language, while China has some 50,000, but just few thousand are used in everyday life?

What country has discovered that the island of Greenland surrendered an average of 150,000,000,000 tons of ice over each of the four summers from 2005 to 2008?

What country, in 2008, gave over $800,000,000 in aid to Ethiopia: $460,000,000 for food, $350,000,000 for AIDs treatment, and just $7,000,000 for agricultural development?

What country's people spend over $2,000,000,000 for anti-perspirants and deodorants per year?

What country reduced their maternal mortality rate from 376 per 100,000 in the 1950s to thirty-seven in 1960 and to just over fifteen in the early 21st Century?

What country had a President who named his three hounds Drunkard, Tipler, and Tipsy?

What country had a President who had a Bull Terrier, a badger, a toad, a pig, and some snakes as pets?

What country had about 190,000 private contractors in the Iraqi war zone at the outbreak of the war . . . just about as many as military personnel?

What country had over 2,100,000 households that had to replace computers because of viruses, spyware, and email scams during 2007 and 2008?

What country has people who pay over $43,000 in additional interest on a thirty-year loan for a $300,000 home, when their FICA score is 625 instead of 721?

What country has radon as the second most cause of lung cancer, and kills some 21,000 per year?

What country has over 700 hospital patients who have surgical objects left in them after their surgeries, per year?

What country has hospitals that make mistakes in some 2,400,000 patients yearly that cause additional care, and the hospitals bill Medicare or the insurance companies for the care needed to recover from those mistakes?

What country has "radiation portal monitors" that are intended to sniff out someone smuggling in "dirty bombs," that have examined 270,000,000 vehicles that resulted in 1,500,000 alarms, but not a single one turned out to be a terrorist threat?

What country has installed devices intended to alert on any high radiation at Canadian and Mexican border crossings, yet the vast majority of alarms have been on granite, bananas, kitty litter, tile, and people who have undergone medical procedures with nuclear isotopes?

What country spent $737,000,000 in 2003 on construction and equipping the Afghan Army, and by 2007 the spending increased to $10,000,000,000?

What country had a President who installed solar panels on the roof of the White House, only to have President Reagan have them removed when he took office?

What country has an Ivy League University that can boast that every President since 1988 has earned a degree there?

What country's top two Ivy League Universities, who normally charge incoming freshmen around $50,000 per year to attend, in 2008 accepted incoming students that had family incomes of about $40,000, at a yearly cost of just around $4,000?

What country's real wages have been on a steady decline since the 1970s?

What country has performed over 40,000,000 abortions since it was made legal?

What country has learned that there were some 880,000,000 international arrivals worldwide in 2007 and just 20,000,000 of them had their passports screened against Interpol's data base that would have revealed some of the 15,000,000 stolen documents?

What country has just a limited number of shipyards that can build those $700,000,000 offshore drilling rigs, and it usually takes up to ten years before the oil begins to flow?

What country increased its total credit card debt by 50 percent between 2000 and 2008?

What country has a paper mill that turns over 1,000 miles of paper a day in rolls wider than a two lane road, and burns some 400,000 barrels of fuel oil per year?

What country has about 65,000 undocumented immigrant students who graduate from high school each year?

What country has about 1,500,000 people with Parkinson's disease and 60,000 new cases diagnosed each year?

What country has a company that became famous for supplying heart pacemakers to people, and now is developing a device that is embedded into the chest and has wires leading directly into the brain?

What country set up lines to manufacture televisions in the 1970s for about $2,000,000, and in 2008 to do the same thing for flat-screen displays cost $3,500,000,000?

What country lost 773 bicyclists in 2006 due to accidents, and tens of thousands of injuries?

What country had a study that showed bicycle fatalities were eleven times higher than car fatalities, per mile traveled?

What country had a study that revealed the rate of pedestrian fatalities associated with walking on the sidewalk was thirty-six times higher than car fatalities?

What country has 696,000 college students who are assaulted yearly by other students who had been drinking?

What country has over 1,700 alcohol-related deaths of college students, yearly?

What country has over 97,000 rapes and sexual assaults of college students due to drinking alcohol, yearly?